Bill Davidson

Symbolic interactionism

D0777871

Monographs in Social Theory

Editor: Arthur Brittan, *University of York*

Titles in the Series

Barry Barnes   *Scientific knowledge and sociological theory*

Zygmunt Bauman   *Culture as praxis*

Keith Dixon   *Sociological theory*

Bernard N. Meltzer, John W. Petras and Larry T. Reynolds
Symbolic interactionism

Anthony D. Smith   *The concept of social change*

A catalogue of books in other series of Social Science books
published by Routledge & Kegan Paul will be found at the end of
this volume.

Bernard N. Meltzer

John W. Petras

Larry T. Reynolds

Symbolic interactionism

Genesis, varieties and criticism

Routledge & Kegan Paul

Boston, London and Henley

First published in 1975
by Routledge & Kegan Paul Ltd
9 Park Street
Boston, Mass. 02108, USA,
39 Store Street, London WC1E 7DD and
Broadway House, Newtown Road,
Henley-on-Thames, Oxon RG9 1EN
Set in Linotype Juliana
and printed in USA by
Vail-Ballou Press, Inc., Binghamton, New York
Reprinted and first published as a paperback 1977
Reprinted in USA 1980
Copyright Bernard N. Meltzer, John W. Petras, Larry T. Reynolds
1975
No part of this book may be reproduced in
any form without permission from the
publisher, except for the quotation of brief
passages in criticism

ISBN 0 7100 8055 7 (c)
ISBN 0 7100 8056 5 (p)

Contents

To our parents—
Anna Kemper Meltzer
Philip Meltzer
Angeline Sedlar Petras
John Petras
Helen I. Reynolds
Roland F. Reynolds

Preface

In brief and broad summary, the perspective known as symbolic interactionism comprises the following basic ideas: The influence that stimuli have upon human behavior is shaped by the context of symbolic meanings within which human behavior occurs. These meanings emerge from the shared interaction of individuals in human society. Society itself is constructed out of the behavior of humans, who actively play a role in developing the social limits that will be placed upon their behavior. Thus, human behavior is not a unilinear unfolding toward a predetermined end, but an active constructing process whereby humans endeavor to 'make sense' of their social and physical environments. This 'making sense' process is internalized in the form of thought; for thinking is the intra-individual problem-solving process that is also characteristic of inter-individual interaction. In thinking, then, there occurs an interaction with oneself. In light of the foregoing, any complete understanding of human behavior must include an awareness of this covert dimension of activity, not simply the observation of overt behavior.

Our intention in writing this monograph has been to accomplish three objectives: (1) to answer the question, what is symbolic interactionism? (2) to describe the major varieties of the interactionist perspective; and (3) to present, and evaluate, criticisms of the perspective. In line with these objectives, the monograph is organized into three major sections.

In chapter 1, we have stated the essential components of symbolic interactionism as a general perspective on human behavior and social life. Included is a consideration of the major ideas found in the basic writings of the perspective's leading figure, George Herbert Mead. While most sociological treatments of Mead's theories of behavior have concentrated upon his psychology with little reference to his philosophy, we have included a discussion of the essential elements of his philosophical system. Furthermore, we have dealt with philosophical pragmatism in our discussion of the intellectual antecedents of symbolic interactionism. Finally, by looking at the relevance of the works of W. James, J. M. Baldwin, J. Dewey, C. H. Cooley, and W. I. Thomas, we have examined the genesis of interactionism in relation to the mainstream of sociological theory at the time it arose.

We believe that symbolic interactionism has too long been considered a relatively homogeneous, or monolithic, orientation. So, chapter 2 describes and analyzes what we conceive to be the diverse schools of thought within the perspective. These schools, or varieties, are shown to have differing historical and intellectual roots, which are situated in varying organizational settings. Our attention has been directed chiefly to the following schools: the Chicago and Iowa schools, the dramaturgical approach, and ethnomethodology. Accordingly, our analysis has taken the form of demonstrating the substantive and methodological differences among these schools and examining the context of the larger social and organizational forces which gave rise to them and continue to sustain them.

In chapter 3, we have made a significant departure from other works concerned with symbolic interactionism as a general perspective on human and social behavior. We have incorporated in this chapter a comprehensive survey of criticisms of the perspective. In this application of reflexive sociology, we have treated the criticisms of both non-interactionists and interactionists. The criticisms comprehend both the conventional theoretical and methodological issues and, in addition, certain ideological issues.

We wish to acknowledge our indebtedness to the various mentors and colleagues who initiated and sustained our interest in the symbolic interactionist orientation: Herbert Blumer (University of California–Berkeley) and Joseph Zygmunt (University of Connecticut), who introduced two of us to the perspective; Carl Couch (University of Iowa) and Robert Stewart (University of South Carolina), former colleagues at Central Michigan University, who familiarized two of us with the Iowa brand of interactionism, and Ted Vaughan (University of Missouri), who stimulated the interest of one of us in a critical approach to interactionism.

B. N. M.
J. W. P.
L. T. R.

chapter 1

The genesis of symbolic interactionism

It is difficult to define what constitutes symbolic interactionism as a theoretical perspective in sociology. While many contemporary sociologists think of this perspective as a unitary approach, some variants have been identified (Kuhn, 1964; Vaughan and Reynolds, 1968; Tucker and Stoeckel, 1969; Meltzer and Petras, 1970; Overington, 1971; Reynolds and McCart, 1972; Petras and Meltzer, 1973). On the other hand, regardless of the varying ways in which symbolic interactionism has been interpreted, most of those identifying with the perspective trace its principal origins to the works of G. H. Mead (especially, 1934).

Mead's ideas have been expounded by several sociologists throughout the years, and the acquaintance of most contemporary sociologists with his works has come through the teaching and writings of his best known student, H. Blumer. As interpreted by Blumer, interactionism consists of three basic premises (1969: 2–6).

First, human beings act towards things on the basis of the meanings that the things have for them. Secondly, these meanings are a product of social interaction in human society. Thirdly, these meanings are modified and handled through an interpretive process that is used by each individual in dealing with the things he/she encounters. The historical underpinnings of these three premises are found not only in the works of Mead, but also in C. H. Cooley's theory of society, J. Dewey's formulation of the concept of habit, and W. I. Thomas' notion of 'the definition of the situation' (Cooley, 1902; Dewey, 1922; Thomas, 1923).

Thus, 'symbolic interaction' is the interaction that takes place among the various minds and meanings that characterize human societies. It refers to the fact that social interaction rests upon a taking of oneself (self-objectification) and others (taking the role of the other) into account (see also Swanson, 1968). It is on the basis of the earlier

1

works of W. James, C. H. Cooley, J. Dewey, W. I. Thomas, and G. H. Mead, as well as several later works in the interactionist tradition (Shibutani, 1961; Rose, 1962; Duncan, 1968; Lindesmith and Strauss, 1968; Blumer, 1969; Manis and Meltzer, 1972), that the interactionist image of human beings can be constructed. The ideological theoretical bias that is present in this image will be discussed in a later section of this work.

Perhaps the most basic element in the image is the idea that the individual and society are inseparable units. While it may be possible to separate the two units analytically, the underlying assumption is that a complete understanding of either one demands a complete understanding of the other. Coupled with this assumption is the belief that the inseparability of the individual and society is defined in terms of a mutually interdependent relationship, not a one-sided, deterministic one. Society is to be understood in terms of the individuals making it up, and individuals are to be understood in terms of the societies of which they are members.

In the interactionist image, human beings are defined as self-reflective beings. Human beings are organisms with selves, and behavior in society is often directed by the self. The behavior of men and women is 'caused' not so much by forces within themselves (instincts, drives, needs, etc.), or by external forces impinging upon them (social forces, etc.), but what lies in between, a reflective and socially derived interpretation of the internal and external stimuli that are present. In turn, this idea is related to another aspect of the interactionist image of men and women: the social origins of the self and human nature.

The interactionist view of human nature is built upon Cooley's dictum (1909:22) that human nature is a group nature, as well as the idea that the self is a process that emerges out of the people. There is, as will be seen later, a tendency in the works of Cooley and Mead to emphasize the co-operative processes in social life because of the interest in self genesis in the child. This is in contrast to other interactionists, e.g. W. I. Thomas, who in his concern with the changes that occur in the developed self of the adult, concentrated upon the disorganizational elements of social life and the role these played in generating conflict and change within the adult personality.

In the interactionist perspective, the individual is seen as existing in dual systems—what Mead referred to as sociality (1932:77). Humans are both determined and determiners. Thus, there is a tendency in interactionism to relegate the role of the social order to that of co-determination, i.e. the social order is considered no more important than the individual, who often creates the influences that are felt within the context of his/her social environment. Since much of the environment's influence is experienced in the form of social meanings, and meanings are learned by individuals in social interaction, behavior is constructed and circular, not predetermined and released. We shall now proceed with a more detailed discussion of the works of the early interactionists and the role that they played in the development of interactionism to its present form.

WILLIAM JAMES (1842–1910)

W. James ranks as one of the most underrated figures in the development of American social psychology. His monumental two-volume work, *Principles of Psychology* (1890), set forth a theory of behavior which indirectly served to strengthen the slowly developing psychological foundations of American sociology that had been originally laid by L. Ward some seven years previously (see especially Petras, 1966; 1970b).[1] Three of the concepts that were dealt with by James in this work proved to be especially relevant for the subsequent development of symbolic interactionism. These were 'habit,' later to be popularized through the writings of J. Dewey; 'instinct,' destined to become the center of controversy in sociological theories of motivation; and 'self,' which was to become the focal point for the majority of works emerging from the symbolic interactionist tradition in American sociology.

According to James, any analysis of the concept of instinct must account for its interrelationship with 'habits.' This view was characteristic of the continual emphasis given to a bond that was perceived to exist between the physiological, phylogenetic, and social natures of human beings. Unlike many later authors who were to develop instinct theories of motivations, James maintained the necessity of understanding how instincts are modified and inhibited by socially learned habits.

An instinct, James wrote (1890 : 383):

is usually defined as the faculty of acting in such a way as to produce certain ends, without foresight of the ends, and without previous education in the performance.

But that which James referred to as 'blind instinct' played only a minor role in his analyses. James tied the social conditioning of instincts to the capability of the human brain to engage in higher mental activities, e.g. memory. Since the human organism is capable of memory, the repetition of what was once instinctual behavior can call to mind the performance of the act at that previous time. Behavior of this type (1890 : 390):

> *must cease to be blind after being repeated*, and must be accompanied with foresight of its 'end' just so far as that end may have fallen under the animal's cognizance.

Thus, the number of instincts characteristic of any species may have little relationship to the complexity of the behavior; especially in the species *homo sapiens*, attention should be focused upon the number of *repeated* behavioral experiences that are traceable to a particular instinct. James goes on to say (1890 : 402):

> most instincts are implanted for the sake of giving rise to habits, and . . . this purpose once accomplished, the instincts themselves, as such, have no *raison d'être* in the physical economy, and consequently fade away.

This view became reflected in the writings of the interactionists and was characteristic of the tradition when H. Blumer coined the term 'symbolic interaction' (1938 : 153):

> The infant is recognized to be very active, and consequently, to have impulses (such as the thirst impulse) which occasion it distress and consequently stir it into activity. These impulses, however, are regarded as being plastic and unchannelized, that is, as not being directed toward any specific goal. The infant has no idea or image of 'what it wants,' but merely experiences discomfort and distress under the influence of an impulse. This impulse gains expression in its emotional behavior and random activity. According to this view, the development of the infant into childhood and adulthood is fundamentally a matter of forming organized or concerted activity in place of its previously random activity, and of channelizing its impulses and giving them goals or objectives. This view, then, like the previous one, recognizes original nature to be important, but not determinate of its subsequent development. It emphasizes the nature of the child, the plasticity of this nature, and the impor-

tance of the unformed impulse. It is substantially the view taken by the group of social psychologists who may be conveniently labeled 'symbolic interactionists.'

In turn, habits arise from past experiences and serve to influence the direction of original instincts in a way that James formulates under a 'law of inhibition by habit' (1890:394):

> When objects of a certain class elicit from an animal a certain sort of reaction, it often happens that the animal becomes partial to the first specimen of the class on which it has reacted, and will not afterward react on any other specimen.

The plasticity of original instincts can also be seen in James' 'law of transitiveness;' i.e. 'many instincts ripen at a certain age and then fade away' (1890:398).

James' attribution of instincts to human make-up did not represent an attempt to arrive at some ultimate cause of motivation at the expense of overly simplifying the complexities of human behavior. Rather, according to him, many human mental capabilities exist *because of* the large number of instinctive impulses that have been implanted; leading to a complication, not simplification, of human behavior. In a statement that remained relatively unelaborated until taken up by J. Dewey some years later, James wrote that instincts (1890:392):

> contradict each other—'experience' in each particular opportunity of application usually deciding the issue. The *animal that exhibits them loses the instinctive demeanor* and appears to lead a life of hesitation and choice, an intellectual life, *not however because he has no instincts—rather because he has so many that they block each other's path* [see also Dewey, 1925].

As set forth in 1890, James' conceptualization of a social self in humans revealed a great deal of sophistication in understanding the relationships between the individual and social groups as being of an interactive nature. In later years, the interests of sociology were to be expressed in the concern for social reform and social problems (O'Kelly and Petras, 1970). American psychology, on the other hand, developed its interests with respect to personality growth and conditions perceived to be influential in affecting human behavior. The interest in the concept of personality led many psychologists to an interest in exploring the interactive nature of the individual and group relationship before such an interest was expressed in sociology. It is for this reason that psychologists such as W. James and, as will be seen later, J. M. Baldwin, are important in understanding the subsequent development of symbolic interactionism in early American sociology.

For James, the general concept of self referred to 'the sum total of all that the individual can call his' (1890:291). Within this general definition, which was intended to cover several areas of human life, James listed the four separate selves of humans (1890:292): a material self, a social self, a spiritual self, and pure ego (see also Davis, 1909). At the time, a significant advance made by James was the removal of the concept of self from the purely metaphysical realm and the view of at least some aspects of it as derived from interaction processes in the social environment. James defined the social self in the following manner (1890:294):

> Properly speaking, a man has as *many social selves as there are individuals who recognize him* and carry an image of him in their mind. To wound any one of these images of his, is to wound him. But as the individuals who carry the images fall naturally into classes, we may practically say that he has as many different social selves as there are distinct *groups* of persons about whose opinion he cares.

As the need in humans to enhance the social self is continually evident, James encountered little difficulty in locating its origin in instinct (1890:308):

> That the direct social self-seeking impulses are probably pure instinct is easily seen. The noteworthy thing about this desire to be 'recognized' by others is that its strength has little to do with the worth of the recognition computed in sensational or rational terms.[2]

The degree to which this inherent need is actualized depends upon an interactive relationship between the objective social stimuli and the subjective aspirations of the individual. James proposed that the degree of self-esteem enjoyed by any one individual can be represented by the ratio of success (the objective social factor), to pretensions (the subjective factor). A person with few pretensions and great successes will enjoy high self-esteem. On the other hand, a person with many pretensions but little success will experience little self-esteem (1890 : 310).

While most of our discussion thus far has centered around those elements of James' work which have direct relevance for the development of symbolic interactionism in American sociology, there is another aspect of his work that is equally important for understanding the congruity between pragmatism, as seen by the early interactionists, and the general image of men and women in society that was characteristic of their approach. We are referring to the pragmatist's definition of human beings as active, creative beings who could play a conscious role in the control of their own destinies. James was one of the first and most vocal critics of H. Spencer and the Spencerians, who, in the pragmatic view, conceptualized behavior within the constraints of social and geographical determinism. What becomes apparent in these critiques is the fact that they served to crystallize the interactive nature of James' theories with respect to the individual-and-society relationship. For, rather than establishing a polemical stance and defining individuals as autonomous in response to the Spencerians, James maintained a position that was intermediary between the two extremes·(see especially 1880; 1897).

A theme reiterated in attacks upon the Spencerians is the implicit fatalism prevalent in their writings. It appears that this opposition served as the framework within which James developed his philosophy of pragmatism : a philosophy where the potentialities of the individual living within the environment were to be realized by applying, scientifically, knowledge of the relationship which existed between the individual and his environment (see especially James, 1907; Brotherton, 1943; Overington, 1971). This philosophy served to tie together the works of James, Dewey, Mead, and Cooley, and it expressed itself in several shared areas of interest.

For the pragmatist, human nature was viewed as grounded in the potential creativity of each human being. This potential could be actualized only in interaction with others in the social order. Thus, the creativity of human beings was not seen to be suppressed by the social order, but was seen as being expressed only through the social order. 'Truth' and 'goodness' were considered social constructs that emerge out of a continually changing social environment. The means and ends of any action cannot be separated, as they are interdependent elements of a continuous behavorial pattern. In a sense, the pragmatists sought to establish social conditions which were most likely to develop the individual potential present in any society at any one time.

Pragmatism, especially as manifested in the psychology of James, provided the basis for an image of humans that was congruent with the developing interactionist perspective.[3]

CHARLES HORTON COOLEY (1864–1929)

A sociologist, Cooley spent his entire academic career at the University of Michigan, but is still considered to be a member of the Chicago school.[4] While a student, he studied under J. Dewey, and the latter's influence upon his theories is quite evident, especially those aspects which deal with the nature of society. Although he is best remembered today for the concepts of 'the primary group' and 'the looking-glass self,' Cooley perceived his major contribution to be his theory of the mental nature of human society (Cooley, 1930; Jandy, 1942).

As will be seen later, the interactionism that developed out of the works of Mead and Dewey was rooted in an understanding of the bases of individual behavior in human society and, as already seen in W. James, intertwined with philosophical concerns. Cooley expanded upon this and, in the sociological, rather than philosophical or psychological, tradition utilized the concept of group and emphasized the role that social entities played in shaping the motivational bases of the behavior of individuals in society. In doing this Cooley had hoped to develop a new theory of human society, and, to this end, detailed the corresponding need for a new methodology which would aim at an understanding of human behavior in the context of society. While taken for granted today, this approach distinguished Cooley from the mainstream of early American sociology (Bodenhafer, 1920–1: 457):

> To attempt to approach the study of society, as Ward did for instance, from the standpoint of the individual, and then attempt to create a social superstructure on the basis of that individual approach is an abstraction that the facts do not warrant. From the beginning, according to Cooley, there must have been a group situation. It is the fundamental hypothesis upon which he constructs his whole subsequent thought [see also Mead, 1934:50].

In the pragmatic tradition, Cooley's works were guided by a consideration of life's practical problems encountered in a developing industrial society. In fact, all of Cooley's writings impart the impression that his sociological theorizing on the structure and organization of society was guided by moral principles derived from the pragmatic tradition, and these, in turn, were tempered by the reality of social life as interpreted in his sociological theories (Hinkle, 1967; Petras, 1968d).

Cooley believed that any valid explanation of human society had to account for two of its unique properties. These were, on the one hand, its organic nature, and on the other hand, its mental nature. As a structure, a society took on the properties of an organism and was to be analyzed in terms of its organic nature (1918 : 28):

> It is a complex of forms or processes each of which is living or growing by interaction with the others, the whole being so unified that what takes place in one part affects all the rest. It is a vast tissue of reciprocal activity, differentiated into innumerable systems, some of them quite distinct, others not readily traceable, and all interwoven to such a degree that you see different systems according to the point of view you take [see Hamilton, 1931].

As social organization, society was seen as existing in the minds of the particular individuals constituting the social unit, and this makes society 'real' to its members. In actuality, there is no 'mind of society,' but many different minds that exist through a sharing of expectations and patterns of behavior, thereby providing the 'glue' which holds the larger organization together (1909 : 4):

> Not in agreement but in organization, in the fact of reciprocal influence or causation among its parts, by virtue of which everything that takes place in it is connected with everything else, and so is an outcome of the whole. . . . This differentiated unity of mental or social life . . . is what I mean . . . by social organization.

In his discussion on the conceptualization of the social organization of society, Cooley provided excellent indications of the role he foresaw for interactionism as a framework through which social reality was to be interpreted. The role of interaction is that of a mediating bond between social environments and individuals, and it is this role that must be scrutinized to obtain an understanding of the mutual interdependence of these two entities in human society (see especially 1918 : 165). Cooley pointed out that the social environment may not be 'bad' in order to have a 'bad influence' upon the individual. Also, a 'bad influence' may be felt from a 'good' environment simply because of the manner in which it is perceived by the individuals who live in that environment. The social scientist, therefore, must continually guard against placing his interpretations of social phenomena 'on top of' the interpretations that are lived as part of the social experience by the participants in the behavior. To this end, Cooley urged the adoption of a methodology that he labelled 'sympathetic introspection,' a methodology that did not settle for observations of external behavior, but attempted to tap the meaning and interpretations of the participants (1926; 1902:84). All conditions of society are natural to it, according to Cooley—the 'degenerate' side as well as the 'normal' side. In the analysis of social problems, therefore, the social scientist is to concern himself/herself less with the search for the 'causes' of behavior than with a concern for the interdependent links that exist between various organic units constituting the group as a whole. In turn, intelligent planning for the future rests upon this principle of mutual interdependence, rather than upon causality.

If the immediate nature of society is to be found in the bonds which exist because of the ideas that individuals have of one another, an understanding of society must be directed towards these bonds. While those non-mental factors which act upon human beings are not unimportant, they are not as important as those constituting the core. The former were referred to by Cooley as the material facts of society, the latter as the social facts. The expression of this general perspective took place through the building of certain concepts which have become indispensable to the interactionist tradition. The remainder of our discussion of Cooley will focus upon these concepts.

The concept of 'the primary group' can serve as a convenient organizational element. It, along with the concepts of 'human nature' and 'the looking-glass self,' form a triadic relationship that underlies Cooley's work on the nature of the relationship between the individual and society.

Chapter III of *Social Organization* (1909:23) begins with the following well-known statement:

> By primary groups I mean those characterized by intimate face-to-face association and co-operation. They are primary in several senses, but chiefly in that they are fundamental in forming the social nature of the ideals of individuals.

The result of intimate face-to-face interaction within such groups is the development of a feeling that Cooley describes as 'we.' It is a feeling whereby the individual, through his/her emotional and bodily feelings, comes to identify himself/herself as an indispensable part of the larger unit. Harmony need not be present, as the primary group represents a microcosm of the larger society, and the essential ingredient is that of the sharing of *expectations*. Why are such groups primary? First of all, Cooley claims, it is through such groups that the individual develops his/her first contacts with the larger society. Secondly, although one's relationship to the group can and does change over time, the changes are not the same, nor to the same degree as those changes which characterize the social relationships in groups that do not maintain the same grip upon the individual's feelings and attention. He goes on to note that it is not at all uncharacteristic for one's sense of worth and feelings to be taken directly from such a group, and, as W. James had pointed out earlier (see page 6), an assault upon the group is often interpreted as an assault upon the self. How then does the concept of human nature tie into that of the primary group?

The nature of human nature had always fascinated the pragmatists and early social behaviorists.[5] No doubt, this was in large part due to the fact that their particular view of individual and social behavior emerged from the framework established by the older nature v. nurture debate that had begun with the publication of Galton's work on genius. In his earlier works, e.g. *Human Nature and the Social Order*, Cooley spoke of human nature as existing on three different levels. He referred, first of all, to a level that was, for the most part, strictly hereditary. He spoke of human nature, secondly, in terms that were closer to the later development of symbolic interactionism, especially with reference to the role that was played by biology in the motivation of behavior. This was a nature that was modified slowly and was stable, for the most part, except for changes that took place in the evolutionary process (see also Dewey, 1910; Mead, 1936). Finally, according to Cooley, there is a human nature that is more social in nature, and this particular level begins to occupy more and more of his attention in later works. This is the human nature that develops within primary groups, and it is here that a link is provided between the three concepts of primary group, human nature, and looking-glass self. This is the human nature that is characterized not only by the acquisition of ethical standards, but, more importantly, by the development of a sense of self that reflects the definitions of the society as interpreted by the primary groups. At this level human nature is most flexible and, consequently, most susceptible to social influences. It is here that human nature can be seen in its principal aspect, that of *plasticity*, or what Cooley calls 'teachability.'

Thus, human nature is characterized by a plasticity which is formed in the primary group. Any attempt at successful social reform and planning in society must be aimed at the values of the individuals involved, as they provide an inextricable tie to the social situations in which individuals find themselves (see especially 1902, 1909, 1918).

His earlier perspective on the development of human nature always led Cooley to caution against the complete dismissal of biological and hereditary factors in behavior. The summing up of the relationship between the social, biological, and primary group influences upon human behavior is found in the third concept of the triad, the looking-glass self.

Cooley's theory of the looking-glass self owes much to the earlier work of J. M. Baldwin, a debt explicitly acknowledged by Cooley. While space here does not permit a full discussion of these earlier theoretical formulations, we should like to mention several features which were especially influential upon the theories of Cooley and, as will be seen, the later theory developed by Mead (see also Petras, 1968c; Baldwin, 1895, 1897, 1902).

All but forgotten today, J. M. Baldwin's theory of the development of the self in the child represented a major advance over the theories of W. James, who, as already demonstrated, was one of the major sources of inspiration for the early interactionists. Rather than speaking of the social self as simply one segment of a larger self in human beings, Baldwin claimed that the total self was an undifferentiated self—a social self. In discussing the development of the self in the child, Baldwin emphasized the relationship between the objective (social) and subjective (individual)—the interaction between society and the mind—and formulated what he believed to be the three major processes of self-development in the child: the projective, subjective, and ejective stages.

The projective stage referred to the level at which consciousness of others develops. In becoming aware of others, the child learns to categorize them on the basis of his/her past experiences with them. For example, seeing the mother enter the room at regular intervals over time gives rise to a set of anticipations and perceptions which differ from those evoked when a stranger enters the room. The subjective stage characterizes the level at which self-consciousness develops. The child begins, in Baldwin's words, 'a career of imitation.' The ejective process refers to the child's 'ejecting' of his/her own feelings and subjective interpretations into others. It represents an elementary form of empathy, and it provides a foundation on which Cooley's methodology of sympathetic introspection and Mead's theory of role-taking rest. These processes occur within the context of the 'dialectic of personal growth' that Baldwin believed characterized a life-time give-and-take relationship constituting the individual and society bond.

For Cooley, the distinguishing mark of the human child at birth was its tremendous capacity for social learning. Social experiences, as mediated through the early social groups, the primary groups, begin to shape the child into a moral entity and give a particular direction to the development of the self-concept. While there are certain overriding expectations, patterns of behavior, values, etc. which are dictated by the society at large, their influence upon the individual is, for the most part, tempered by the early social and primary groups. The actual 'feeling' of a sense of self appears to develop parallel to a feeling of power and control by the child, who soon learns the ways in which one can manipulate the social and physical environment. Finally, the self becomes lodged in one's life experiences through the development of an individual identity. The identity is obtained when the child becomes aware of the fact that the picture of who he/she is reflects the imaginations of others concerning him/her. Thus, as with the bonds of the social order, the self exists in the minds of the members of society and, for Cooley, constitutes an 'imaginative fact' (1902:86):

> Persons and society must be studied primarily in imagination. It is true, *prima facie*, that the best way of observing things is that which is most direct; and I do not see how we can hold that we know persons directly except as imaginative ideas in the mind.

In the processes that constitute the dialectic of personal growth as Baldwin characterized it, it is the early primary groups that play the major role in the fostering of intelligence, the growth of a sense of morality, and the development of human nature. The function of this dialectic in the genesis of the self and the corresponding processes of development can be summarized as teaching the child the ways in which one acquires a self and identity.

On the basis of the rather unsystematic observation of his own children, Cooley was to reach a conclusion that became an integral aspect of the later theories of Mead. That is, the child develops an awareness of other selves before there is an awareness of his/her own. That this may be too simplistic an explanation has been challenged in recent literature. There is evidence, also, to indicate that, contrary to Cooley and, even more so, Mead, language is not necessarily the principal element in the transmission of the sense of self (see for example Denzin, 1972; Lanstein, 1973).

In addition to the triadic relationship among the major concepts of Cooley, we must mention the close relationship between his perspective on society and the pragmatic tradition of which his work was a part. As with all the pragmatists, Cooley did not regard his theories of human behavior as having no reference to the practical. Indeed, if any one characteristic can be used to tie the varying approaches of the early interactionists to one another, it was the view that their theories of individual and social behavior could be applied to the larger macrocosm from which they were originally derived for use in intelligent social planning. This was possible, according to these thinkers, because their theories of human behavior described processes that were a major part of the social order and the larger context of society (see for example Mead, 1899).

The concepts of freedom and individuality were important to the early interactionists. In terms of their view of the relationship between the individual and society, it was only within the social order that creativity, as a part of individuality, could achieve its fullest potential. This was in contrast to those theorists who operated from an individual-generated perspective. For in the latter view, where human nature is seen as primarily inborn and non-social in nature, society and the social order are seen as major obstacles in the search for individuality and freedom. Indeed, as with Freud, who operated from such a perspective, society is considered a negative influence upon human behavior—so much so that human nature is twisted, perverted, and often warped in such a way that its worst influences come to the fore, forced there by the unnatural restraints of the society.[6]

In pointing out the triadic relationship among the major concepts of Cooley's theory of individual and social behavior, several things are to be noted. First of all, each of the concepts is to be understood only with reference to the others. Secondly, criticisms of the 'romanticism' of Cooley's works often miss this point. Cooley did not rest with the assertion that primary groups would remain unchanged in a changing society. Rather, he contended that in order for the sense of self to continue with reference to the larger social order, it was necessary that new primary groups develop which could nourish the changing self in a modern society (see especially 1918 : 143 and 381). The problems of modern development are inextricably bound up with the lack of recognition of the plasticity of human beings. A vital, changing society depends upon the full usage of this potential human nature, and, as we have pointed out, this is always developed with reference to the dialectic of personal growth—a process that is defined in terms of change and conflict.

JOHN DEWEY (1859–1952)

A philosopher and psychologist, J. Dewey was a member of the Chicago school and is best remembered today for his work in educational reform, but little remembered in sociology for the role he played in the development of what was to be labeled symbolic interaction theory (Petras, 1968b). Dewey began his philosophical career as a Hegelian, but made a dramatic turn to the pragmatic view of the world after coming into contact with the works of W. James. He was a close friend of G. H. Mead, and they shared many features of their theories of individual and social behavior, especially those which dealt with the acquisition of thought and the development of the mind in human society. As for Dewey's sociology, no theorist or sociologist since the time of L. Ward was as adamant as he in advocating the principle of social telesis.

Dewey's writings in philosophy, psychology, and social theory can be systematized around the concepts and concerns that characterized early American sociology. In philosophy, Dewey was most critical of the fact that the experience of philosophizing held little practical value in aiding men and women to meet the ever-changing demands upon them in their day-to-day living. In psychology, Dewey was most critical of those theories of motivation which ignored the role of social interaction in human behavior (see especially 1896, 1908, 1917a, 1920).

In changing from the perspective of Hegelian idealism to the pragmatism that characterized the thought of W. James, Dewey set out to 'reconstruct' philosophy with the intention of proposing solutions to problems of everyday life. He raised the question as to the validity of the problems discussed by philosophy—a more basic question than simply disagreeing with the solutions which had been offered (1917a:69):

> Faith in the power of intelligence to imagine a future which is the projection of the desirable in the present, and to invent the instrumentalities of its realization, is our salvation. And it is a faith which must be nurtured and made articulate: surely a sufficiently large task for our philosophy.

There is, Dewey wrote, no such thing as 'pure thought' or 'pure reason.' While philosophy has conducted its labors under the guise of a concern with problems and conditions of ultimate reality, it has actually been occupied with the study and dissemination of social values which are an inextricable part of social environments out of which philosophy itself emerges (1915, 1938; Curtis and Petras, 1970). Once the relativity of philosophical systems, as well as the relativity of the problems of philosophy is granted, the reconstruction can begin. The notion of a connection between the relativity of philosophical systems and the social environment had been touched upon briefly by James in his earlier writings, but never developed. Dewey's extension of this idea concentrated upon the areas of logic and ethics.

Dewey's attack upon traditional conceptions of logic was aimed at the belief that one could speak of a system of reality separate and distinct from the individual members of society. In rejecting this view, Dewey noted that the resultant position was one which defined humans, their environment, and their thought as interrelated aspects of a larger whole. The individual was seen to play an important role in the perceiving and 'conditioning' of the things that he/she consequently 'knows' (see especially Fisch, 1950; Aiken, 1962; Barrett, 1962; White, 1963). Thus (Dewey, 1938:65):

> The very fitness of the Aristotelian logical organon in respect to the culture and common sense of a certain group in the period in which it was formulated unfits it to be the logical formulation of not only the science, but even of the common sense of the present cultural epoch.

It should come as no surprise to discover that Dewey believed a metaphysics to be impossible. There can be no knowledge or thinking that precedes the individual as a thinking being, because of the interactional character of all experience in human society. Experience takes the form of providing the conditions under which individuals will develop, a view which had been espoused by James and, as we have seen, by C. H. Cooley. It was a view that is thoroughly consistent with the idea that human society does not restrict creativity and individuality, but allows their development in interactional settings that define them as such. The concept most basic to Dewey's thought on the relationship between the individual and the social group is habit. Dewey's concept of habit is important not only in itself, but also in the sense that it provides us with a convenient indicator for looking at the changes that took place in his thought. As habit moved to occupy more and more of a central position in his thought, its definition changed to reflect his greater concern with the social elements in behavior. In the early book, *Psychology* (1887:112), Dewey referred to habit as a 'form of successive associations where one element reintegrates the next, and so on.' By the time of the publication of *Human Nature and Conduct* (1922:42), Dewey stated that the essence of habit was not repetition, but rather:

an acquired predisposition to *ways* or modes of response, not to particular acts except as, under special conditions, these express a way of behaving. Habit means special sensitiveness or accessibility to certain classes of stimuli, standing predilections and aversions, rather than the bare recurrence of specific acts.

The conditions which constitute habit, however, lie not in the individual, but in the social order. For the most part, this had not been emphasized by the early American sociologists, who tended to operate from an individual-generated perspective and believed that 'habits' could be changed by a concerted effort in the direction of changing the individual, with little reference to the conditions that were present in the social order. But for Dewey (1922:30):

Only when a man can already perform an act of standing straight does he know what it is like to have a right posture and only then can he summon the idea required for proper execution. The act must come before the thought, and a habit before the ability to evoke the thought at will.

The most notable feature of the changing definition of the role of habit in Dewey's philosophy and theory of social behavior is the increasing attention given to the role of social elements in behavior. As already mentioned, James had made use of the concept of habit earlier, in the *Principles of Psychology*. For James, however, the concept was used in explaining the repetitious behavior of individuals in society, even when the behavior acted to their objective detriment—as in his example of the poor nöt rising up against the rich because of the fact that their life was organized around an environmental adjustment that entailed satisfaction with their status (1890:121).

It was one year prior to the publication of his *Psychology* that Dewey began to demonstrate an interest in the role of interaction as an element in explaining human and social behavior. In his revolutionary article, 'The Reflex Arc Concept in Psychology' (1896:357), Dewey attacked the mainstream body of theory in psychology of that time:

> The older dualism between sensation and idea is repeated in the current dualism of peripheral and central structures and functions; the older dualism between body and soul finds a distinct echo in the current dualism of stimulus and response.

In the search for explanations of behavior, psychologists had fallen into the trap of resting their case upon those observable conditions of behavior which appear as most evident at a particular time, i.e. the things which, with reference to the whole range of elements that are present in any behavioral phenomenon, are most easily pigeon-holed (1896:369):

> Sensation as stimulus . . . means simply a function, and it will have its value shift according to the special work requiring to be done. At one moment the various activities of reaching and withdrawing will be the sensation, because they are that phase of activity which sets the problem, or creates the demand for, the next act. . . . Generalized, sensation as stimulus is always that phase of the activity requiring to be defined in order that a co-ordination may be completed. What the sensation will be in particular at a given time, therefore, will depend entirely upon the way in which an activity is being used. It has no fixed quality of its own. The search for the stimulus is the search for the exact conditions

of action; that is, for the state of things which decides how a beginning co-ordination should be completed.

Working within the tradition of functional psychology, Dewey turned his attention to the non-functional conceptualization of the human mind as a fixed unit which could be analyzed as structure. Instead, Dewey proposed that the mind be viewed as function, with 'mind activity' extrapolated from adaptive behavior in an ever-changing environment. This latter view of the human mind is most congenial with attempts at intelligent social planning, according to Dewey, while the former view has had disastrous consequences for reform activities (1917b : 273) :

> The ultimate refuge of the standpatter in every field, education, religion, politics, industrial and domestic life, has been the notion of an alleged fixed structure of the mind. As long as mind is conceived of as an antecedent and ready-made thing, institutions and customs may be regarded as its off-spring. . . . The most powerful apologetics for any arrangement or institution is the conception that it is the inevitable result of fixed conditions of human nature.

Dewey's approach to the study of individual and social behavior imposed upon humans a perspective which defined them as social beings. In turn, he cast the entire perspective of human behavior into a phylogenetic framework which stressed the idea of differentiation in terms of degree, not kind. The relationship between the organism and the social environment becomes manifested in the interaction between the mind and the environment. The ultimate effect of this approach is to erase the superimposed boundaries that are conceived to exist internally in the mind and externally in behavior (see especially 1922 : 30). Activity is to be seen in terms of the integrated nature of mind, body, and environment (1896).

Given the conception of the social nature and bases of the human mind, Dewey follows the pattern of most theorists operating from such a perspective and ties conception to the role of language. Language became, for Dewey, and for Mead as will be seen, the element differentiating between the human and non-human animals on the phylogenetic continuum. It was language that allowed human beings to live a meaningful existence and to conceptualize the ideal in human nature (see also Firestone, 1971). Language was the vehicle that allowed humans to locate the thoughts, feelings, and beliefs acquired from the social environment into their own selves and the selves of others. In other words, the social development of the mind could take place only through communciation.

A major concern in our discussion of Dewey has been to demonstrate the important, but neglected, role he played in the development of the social behaviorism that developed into symbolic interactionism. In an important sense, Dewey, along with Mead, extended the province of psychology into sociology and developed a theory that attempted to use both individual and social elements as the basis for explanations of human behavior. This had an innovating effect upon the theories of motivation that prevailed in sociology and differentiated it from the mainstream of sociological social psychology at the time (Petras, 1966).

In his description of early American sociology, F. House wrote (1936:320):

> Ross's social psychology was a collective psychology or theory of collective behavior. This social psychology of Baldwin, Dewey, Cooley and Mead, in contrast, is a social theory of individual behavior or personality, though it has implications for the interpretations of collective behavior.

In concluding our treatment of Dewey, we shall look at the practical application of his theories through the approach that he took toward the area of social reform. This was the area that captured most of his interest as a pragmatist and, at the same time, it was an area which offers the finest example of how the psychological and sociological strands were tied together.

As previously mentioned, Dewey's advances in the study of social problems are best seen in the application of the concept of habit to the theory of social behavior. Thus, in his view, while social reform is important for the development of a society based upon pragmatic principles, its success requires educational reform—the area for which Dewey is best remembered today. In far too many cases, Dewey remarks (1916:16):

> The activity of the immature human being is simply played upon to secure habits which are useful. He is trained like an animal rather than educated like a human being. His instincts remain attached to his original objects of pain or pleasure.

In Dewey's mind, the dream of a socially planned society, rich in creativity and individuality, could not be realized unless those institutions concerned with the early years of life took on the task of educating individuals to be receptive to the types of changes that would be necessary for such an event to occur. The logical starting point for the beginning of such an awareness was the early school years. The educational system had to become an integral part of the organic whole that constituted the individual's life.

The role of the school system, as envisioned by Dewey, was closely tied to his conception of the role and definition of what should comprise the realm of social science in a modern and changing world. Discounting the view that described social reality in terms of a monostructural society, Dewey clearly reveals his relationship to Cooley (1920:205):

> Society . . . is many associations, not a single organization. Society means association; coming together in joint intercourse and action for the better realization of any form of experience which is augmented and confirmed by being shared. Hence, there are as many associations as there are goods which are enhanced by being mutually communicated and participated in. And these are literally indefinite in numbers.

And, as with Cooley, Dewey's view of society dictated the definition of the social sciences, their methodology, and their picture of social reality. The natural and social sciences differed in terms of the phenomena that are studied. As with philosophy, the defining of the social sciences was to be practicality in the applications of its findings, techniques, and procedures to everyday situations confronted by men and women in society. Rather than construct artificial situations and attempt to study phenomena when they occur within these static boundaries, the social scientist was to study phenomena through instituting deliberate changes into the social body. For, given the nature of human society, it was only in this way that societal change could be studied with reference to the other changes it evoked (see especially Fisch, 1950:21).

The scientific status of the discipline did not determine the time at which sociology would enter upon the path of social planning and reform. Rather, it was through the institution of change and social planning that sociology would achieve its scientific status and, at the same time, justify its worth to a society in need of solutions to the problems of everyday living.

W. I. THOMAS (1863–1947)

The works of W. I. Thomas represent, better than the works of any of the other early interactionists, the attempt to find a theory of motivation that mediated between the individual and social sources of behavior. Thomas began his career by singling out instincts of food and sex as the most basic motivational elements in men and women in society (1895). Later he looked to organic differences between men and women as an explanatory factor (1907), to the concept of 'wishes,' where an attempt was made to combine the social and biological bases of behavior into a single concept for the explanation of motivation (1923), and to the 'definition of the situation,' the concept for which he is best remembered today (1923). Toward the close of his career, his works emphasized the importance of situational influences upon behavior, and he was especially interested in the effects of social disorganization and social change upon the adult personality.[7]

Through the changes in his theories of behavior, his works represent, in microcosm, the changes that were taking place in American sociology, especially with respect to the perspective used in the analysis of motivation. These changes paralleled the changes that were being brought about through the influence of other social behaviorists (Petras, 1970a; see also Boskoff, 1969).

Also, in developing a theory that was consistent with those of the other social behaviorists, Thomas was to provide, through his monumental work with Znaniecki, the first large-scale test of many of the propositions that had been developed with respect to the social nature of the self and the role of society in determining individual behavior (Thomas and Znaniecki, 1918). Thomas' later works, especially, are characterized by an over-riding interest in the interrelationships between the personality, the situation, and sympathetic introspection. In addition, Thomas left his own mark on the development of symbolic interactionism by extending the theory of personality from an emphasis upon childhood to one upon adulthood. Indeed, this may serve as one of the basic differentiating features between the work of Cooley and that of Thomas.

Cooley, with his interest in the genesis of the self in children and the role of society in providing the framework for such development, was led to emphasize the cooperative features of the individual-and-society relationship. Thomas, on the other hand, with his interest in the effect of social change and societal disorganization upon the adult personality, was led to pay particular attention to the conflicting features of the environment, i.e. those features which pressured individuals to reconceptualize 'developed' selves. This interest also helps to account for the diminishing role of the organic factor in Thomas' theories of motivation. For, in the study of adult personalities, the direct influence of inborn characteristics is considered to be of least importance in adulthood, as compared with childhood. It is assumed, for example, that the impulses which play an important role in the life of the infant have been socially modified, and it is possible to look more and more to the social factors for an understanding of the individual's behavior.[8] Although Thomas always maintained an individualistic element in his treatments of motivation, it took on the form of the subjective element in the individual's psychology. In a sense, therefore, it would be correct to say that as Thomas moved towards a greater awareness of the role played by objective factors in behavior, he moved towards a more social-deterministic position. What the direction of his works does indicate is a growing usage of the conception of interaction in his explanations of human and social behavior.

All of the thinkers discussed thus far, including Thomas and, as will be seen, G. H. Mead, took as the foundation of their theories a unique relationship between the individual and society. According to these theories, all humans enter the world as a collection of organic impulses. Thus, these thinkers sought to salvage an important vestige of the theories of motivation that had utilized an individual-generated perspective. Rather than viewing the organic factor in the form of specific instincts that had to be worked out in specific forms of behavior, they emphasized an impulsive and plastic inborn nature which was shaped in such a way by its social environment that its ends came to be defined by the social. It was this plasticity which, as we have already seen in the theories of Cooley, became defined as the basis for human nature itself. As all of the early interactionists pointed out, the exact weight to be given to the organic factor in behavior would never be known, for humans are, from birth to death, social beings. Therefore, even in an attempt to understand the role of organic and individual factors in motivation, men and women must be approached through the social medium of analysis.

We must now look more closely at specific sections of Thomas' works. The earliest aspect of Thomas' individual-generated perspective on motivation was published in 1896. At that time, he concluded that (1896:445):

> food and sex are irreducible factors of social life; and beginning with these we may hope to understand the meaning of the different variables of society: ideas, institutions, beliefs, sentiments, language, arts, literature—and to trace the 'red thread' of consciousness through them.

After food and sex, the dimension that received the most extensive attention in Thomas' early writings on human motivation were inborn, biological differences that exist between the sexes. In a collection of articles exemplifying this particular theory of the various motivational differences between men and women in society, Thomas began his introduction with the following explanatory statement (1907:V):

> While each study is complete in itself, the general thesis running through all of them is the same—that the differences in bodily habit between men and women, particularly the greater strength, restlessness, and motor-aptitude of man, and the more stationary condition of women, have had an important influence on social forms and activities, and on the character and the mind of the two sexes.

If, according to Thomas, we compare the roles of cultural and organic factors in the behavior of men and women, it is necessary to take into account their relative spans in the spectrum of evolutionary history. Those who advocate the notion that the cultural has overtaken the organic as an influence in behavior have lost sight of the fact that the two are not comparable in the historical and evolutionary sense. Through a phylogenetic perspective, Thomas argues, it becomes clear that the period of cultural life in the experience of men and women is minute compared to the period of shared biological heritage. It is, therefore, not at all unreasonable to assume that even though behavior varies between different cultures, there are types of psychic reaction that have been given and fixed for longer periods of time; and, in this sense, men and women can never get away from the original sources of stimulation and response and the role they play in acquired social and human behavior (1907:100). This opposition between the cultural and organic levels of life added another dimension to the writings of Thomas, which tends to complement theories of motivation that cluster around an individual-generated perspective. Society and social norms come to be seen, in the early works, in terms of the negative influences that they have upon individuals. Society is viewed as stifling an inborn individuality in men and women. Indeed, as with Freud (no date; see also Ogburn, 1922; Winston and Ogburn, 1929), the normality of men and women is believed to be threatened by forced living under conditions that are unnatural to the human species. Thomas was, for a considerable length of time, content simply to trace individual social behavior back through the phylogenetic continuum, offering such tracing as an explanation for the presence of the behavior in human society.

The class system of society provides Thomas with yet another example of the conditions that develop when men and women are forced to live an unnatural life by the pressures of a society acting against human nature. Referring to the position of women in society, Thomas writes that observation will bear out the fact that (1906: 36–7):

> The heavy, strong, enduring, patient, often dominant type frequently seen among the lower classes, where alone woman is still enormously functional, is probably a good representative of what the women of our race were before they were reduced by man to a condition of parasitism which, in our middle and so-called higher classes, has profoundly affected their physical, mental, and moral life.

In these early works Thomas patterned his theory of behavior after a search for irreducible 'facts' of motivation. Once these were found, an understanding of society would follow through tracing their manifestations in the social order. It was after the publication of these works, where the individual-generated perspective played the major role, that Thomas formulated the concept of the wishes, a unit of analysis that constituted an attempt to combine both the organic and social factors in behavior (Hinkle, 1963 : 711):

> Each one of . . . the four wishes derives from experience with conscious regulation of one or more inherited affective dispositions. New experience and security come respectively from curiosity and fear. Response and recognition apparently merge from love.

The wishes have been defined as forces which impel towards action (1923 : 4), but not as the causes of behavior (Volkart, 1951 : 16–17).

The concept of the wish parallels closely the idea of what Mead labeled an 'inner condition'—a 'want.' For Mead, the act, as defined in his lectures, is 'a stimulus and response on the basis of an inner condition which sensitizes the system to the stimulus and quickens the response' (Blumer, no date). The wish also parallels J. Dewey's concept of habit; i.e. it takes into account both the individual and social factors in behavior. Through behavior that is under the direction of the wishes, human beings develop habits which persist until something occurs to change the behavior or force a modification of the course it has been taking. Such an event is called a 'crisis,' and it disrupts habits by re-directing the attention that formerly had been focused there by the individual or the group (see also Shibutani, 1961 : 64). By meeting the new needs that are defined in terms of the crisis, individuals and groups exert control over the situation. This view closely matched the pragmatic approach to experience and perception (Thomas, 1909 : 14). Then, there is another (Bogardus, 1940 : 340) :

> lapse into a state of disinterestedness until another disturbance of habit occurs. The new method of control will be imitated. If imitated widely, it will mark a rise in the level of civilization.

The vehicles by which the individual is able to control crises are provided by the society of which he or she is a member. Thus, as with the concept of habit, the conditions of the phenomena are given in the social order and, in combination with the individual, as defined in the pragmatic perspective, act to produce an adjustment to the situation. By studying the processes surrounding crises, the social scientist is looking at the interrelatedness between the individual and the social group. The evolution of Thomas' works to this position, where the social factors are seen as more and more important in his theory of motivation, culminates in the concept of 'the definition of the situation.' Although the concept was developed earlier than that of the wishes, its extensive usage did not occur until later.

Again, one can note similarities with the other early interactionists. In the case of the definition of the situation, there is a close resemblance to the idea of the philosophy of the present as developed by Mead in his discussions of the role of time and emergence in human behavior. For, the concept of the definition of the situation implies, as with Mead's philosophy of the present, that the past and the future are often defined with respect to an emergent present. Terminologically, the relationship to the past is found in the wishes and crises. The relationship to the future is found in what Thomas called the 'as if' behavior of men and women in human society.[9] Individuals, Thomas writes, always act in an 'as if' fashion. That is, there is an effort to define each of the paths of contemplated behavior on the basis of what will result if a person follows one path and not another. This deliberation that takes place prior to any self-determined form of behavior is called the definition of the situation. Thus (Volkart, 1951:30):

> Facts do not have a uniform existence apart from the persons who observe and interpret them. Rather, the 'real' facts are the ways in which different people come to define situations.

This relationship between the individual and facts was also expressed as the relationship between attitudes and values (Thomas and Znaniecki quoted in Barnes, 1922:19):

> A nomothetic social science is possible only if all social becoming is viewed as a product of continual interaction of individual consciousness and objective social reality. In this connection the human personality is both a continually producing factor and a continually produced result of social evolution, and this double relation expresses itself in every elementary and social fact; there can be for social science no change of social reality which is not the common effect of pre-existing social values and individual attitudes acting upon them.

The methodology of human behavior is to aim at tapping both social values, 'any datum having an empirical content accessible to the members of some social group and a meaning with regard to which it is or may be an object of activity,' and attitudes, each of which is a process 'of individual consciousness which determines real or possible activity of the individual in the social world. . . . The attitude is thus the individual counterpart of the social value' (Thomas and Znaniecki, 1918:21 and 22).

We shall now turn our attention to the best-known figure in the development of symbolic interactionism—G. H. Mead.

GEORGE HERBERT MEAD (1863–1931)

Dewey's early work on communication and the ensuing development of his thought were never synthesized into a theoretical system that had any direct influence upon American sociology. Although he influenced several persons individually, his books were more or less neglected within the mainstream of sociology. Ironically, G. H. Mead, a close friend of Dewey, published no books during his lifetime, but has become one of the best-known 'sociologists.' A consequence of the paucity of publication by Mead in the sociological tradition has been the fact that sociologists tend to be familiar with his approach to behavior only through posthumous collections, and an appreciation of the development of his own thought has been lost. Thus, while most sociologists have at least a passing acquaintance with Mead's theory of self, few understand the philosophical and evolutionary context out of which it arose (see Tremmel, 1957; Miller, 1972; Farberman, 1970; Corti, 1973; Miller, 1973a, 1973b; Petras, 1973a).

A further point which has been made, but seldom corrected, is that this limited acquaintance with Mead rests mainly with *Mind, Self and Society* (1934).[10] In this section, we shall treat Mead's theory of the self as the focal point at which he synthesizes his work in the philosophical and psychological traditions. All this leads to the question: why have Mead's theories, particularly the theory of self development, become so well known in sociology? While many observers are content to explain this phenomenon in terms of the group of devoted students who surrounded Mead, we believe there is a more important element involved, one which underlies the devotion of certain students.

The questioning of theories of motivation operating from an individual-generated perspective was reaching its height at the time of Mead's influence at Chicago. In that intellectual climate, Mead's theories provided an excellent alternative to the extremes that were operating from an individual-generated perspective. With the growing awareness of the role that social influences play in combination with perception, there was a need for an explanation of behavioral processes that would incorporate findings from extremes. Mead attempted to account for the ways in which these processes worked in human society, where men and women, given the nature of individual and social life, were both determined and determiners at the same time.

A striking aspect of Mead's work on human behavior is the fact that all of it is conceptualized within a phylogenetic frame of reference. While the early interactionists were influenced by Darwin, none of their theories of individual and social behavior relied as much upon the principles of continuity and flux as those of Mead. Mead's particular usage of the perspective was directed towards that point on the evolutionary continuum where humans became differentiated from the remainder of the animal kingdom. Although Mead's early writings tended to be devoted to more pragmatic issues of educational reform, the early works contain, in non-elaborated form, many of the concepts which were to become linked to those of his theories prominent in the early development of symbolic interactionism. Thus, as suggested elsewhere (Petras, 1973a), the underlying basis for Mead's theories regarding the genesis of the self and the role of society and the mind in human behavior, evolves out of his working within a phylogenetic framework. It was this perspective, coupled with the underlying philosophy of the present and theory of emergence, that established the path upon which his theories run from the level of general concepts to the particular application of these, and the sociological theory of the self can be seen as a particular example of the processes discussed in his works in philosophy and psychology.

The early articles were concerned with the problems that were facing the school systems of the time, especially in the city of Chicago. The earliest article described the necessity of play and spontaneous activity as a basis for the development of the human child in the classroom. Mead wrote that the purpose of the article was to 'criticize the basing, especially of the earlier education of our children, upon . . . the work phase of activity' (1896: 142). Over the next several years, Mead utilized a view of society that defined the institutional relatedness between the different parts with respect to a larger whole. In an article that appeared in 1903, Mead criticized those who viewed the relationship between the school system and the remainder of society solely on the basis of political and economic dependence, i.e. the view which divorced the formal educational process from the everyday world of society, and, instead, viewed the educational process as a separate category in the child's life. In reaction to this view, Mead, as well as Dewey, emphasized the necessity of developing a vocational system which would bring the everyday world of the society closer to the world of the classroom. The vocational network was especially needed to close the gap between reality as perceived in the formal sense through the academic setting and reality as lived by the children of Chicago outside of school. In Mead's view, the immediate task of the educational system was (1907b : 284):

> To use the child's own impulse, his native interests, material which is worthy because it has meaning for him, and the nature for getting technique which springs from interest in what he does, and yet to make felt the authoritative discipline and criticism of human achievement, which is as real a part of the child's normal life as it is of the adult; though the incidence is not the same [see also 1908; 1912a].

It is clear in these articles that Mead was attempting to model the educational system after his conceptualization of what he considered to be the higher processes that governed consciousness in society. Instruction was to become a means of personal intercourse between pupils and instructors, as well as between children themselves. Ideally, the learning situation substitutes 'the converse of concrete individuals for the pale abstractions of thought' (1910a). The relationship to the larger whole of society is crucial, for the child does not develop social nature through learning, but learning presupposes a social nature (1910a : 693).

These early articles help to provide evidence for the fact that Mead's thought evolved out of the pragmatic tradition, and this perspective defined the ways in which he came to define humans with respect to motivation. We can begin a more detailed analysis of these ideas by looking at Mead's conception of mind.

Mead constructed a functional theory of mind that is similar in all important respects to the approach of Dewey. The mind is an instrument which finds its reality in behavioral manifestations. The mind exists not in structure but in conduct that 'is not confined to the individual much less located in the brain. Significance belongs to things in their relationships to individuals. It does not lie in mental processes which are enclosed within individuals' (1922 : 163). The mind is a tool which seeks an adjustive relationship between the individual and his/her environment. The notion that the mind is selective, that it 'uses previous experience to determine the nature of the stimulus attended to' (Bittner, 1931 : 7) follows closely the principles that were laid down in Dewey's reflex arc article. Mead elaborated upon the conception of consciousness, as it is organized in the individual, and stressed the idea of looking at it in terms of its objects and the relations of these objects to conduct (see especially 1912b). Psychology, then, becomes (1934:40):

> not something that deals with consciousness; psychology deals with the experience of the individual in its relation to the conditions under which the experience goes on. It is social psychology where the conditions are social ones. It is behavioristic where the approach to experience is made through conduct.

This relocation of the psychology of the mind into the social environment and away from the individual is based upon Mead's introduction of a theory which attempts to account for the growth of the mind. Mead had been greatly influenced by those of W. Wundt's theories which focus on the concept of the gesture, but he took issue with Wundt's theory of the origin of society, which was based upon the presupposition of the existence of individual minds. Such an explanation is incomplete, according to Mead, because it leaves no explanation for the origin of these minds in individuals. In Mead's view, the minds themselves develop out of, and are part of, a social process that is already present. The origin of the human mind is explained with reference to the interaction processes and communication that are present (1934:50).

While the mind emerges out of social interaction, its high level of development among humans depends upon a condition that represents a synthesis of their biological, psychological, and sociological nature. This process, 'the turning back of the experience of the individual upon himself,' is reflexiveness (1934:134).

Mead's first discussion of the process of reflexiveness was not concerned with a particular ability of the human mind, but was formulated with reference to a general societal process. Thus, Mead does not speak of individual minds, but of mind development in the human species. In this early view, reflective thought is seen as a process of phylogenetic differentiation which contained the key for social reform and reconstruction (1899:371):

> Our reflective consciousness as applied to conduct is, therefore, an identification of our effort with the problem that presents itself, and the developmental process by which it is overcome, and reaches its highest expression in the scientific statement of the problem, and the recognition and use of scientific method and control [see also 1905:405].

Thought, or the process of thinking, was considered a pragmatic endeavor. It represents an internalization of the overt processes which are employed to deal with and mediate the conflicts and blockages at the social level (1900:2):

> All analytic thought commences with the presence of problems . . . it continues always to be an expression of such conflict and the solution of the problems involved. . . . All reflective thought arises out of real problems present in immediate experience, and is occupied entirely with the solution of these problems or their attempted solution. . . . This solution finally is found in the possibility of continuing activity, that has been stopped along new or old lines, when such reflective thought ceases in the nature of the case [see also 1906].

Perception functions as a mediative experience for the individual in the relationship between himself/herself and the social environment. Both thinking and perceiving have instrumental value, and this defines its experiencing by the individual (1907a: 390). Mead accentuates this pragmatic element in perception as a mediating relationship when he writes (1907a: 390):

> Every perceived thing is in so far as perceived a recognized means to a possible end, and there can be no hard and fast line drawn between such perceptual consciousness and the more abstracted processes of so-called reasoning. Any form that perceives is in so far carrying on a process of conscious mediation within its act and conscious mediation is ratiocination.

This perceptual ability of human beings, which is intricately linked with the development of thought processes and thinking ability, can be traced to differentiations in the evolutionary continuum (1907a: 388).

The instrumentality of human behavior which appears at the covert level in the form of thought and perception is paralleled overtly with the 'act'—the fundamental unit of social behavior. The act is a self-contained behavioral process that incorporates the conditions for its genesis and outcome within the process itself. In his lectures, Mead defined the act as 'a stimulus and response on the basis of an inner condition which sensitizes the system to the stimulus and quickens the response' (Blumer, no date). The 'inner condition' originates within the person and then unfolds into the social world where it becomes manifested as social behavior. The initiation of the social act commences with the gesture which outlines the behavior that is to follow. At the individual level, the act begins as an impulse, indicative of Mead's insistence on the fact that any adequate explanation of motivation had to account for the biological, as well as the social, heritage of humans (see also Mead, 1938: 3–25; Shibutani, 1961 : 66).

Shibutani (1961 : 66) notes that the act can be broken down into five important stages and that it proceeds towards the restoration of equilibrium to a dynamic-tension state. We shall look first at the act on the individual level :

Impulse: The individual 'feels hungry.'

Perception: The individual thinks about a steak (or, in another society, he/she may think about grub worms). In other words, that which we imagine as having the ability to satisfy our impulse— hunger—is 'screened' through our perceptual framework on the basis of the cultural definitions of objects considered to be appropriate as food (steak, not grub worms) and on the basis of the individual's own preferences (steak, not chicken).

Manipulation: The individual takes some form of action which ends in eating, or defers gratification by thinking about the fact that he/she will eat later in the day and, through this 'imagined satisfaction,' contains, redirects, and controls the impulse.

Consummation: The act ends : the individual eats the steak (or grub worms) or forgets about the fact that he/she is hungry, or, in the extreme case, dies of starvation. The consummation of the act at the individual level means that 'striving,' as introduced by the original impulse, ceases.

An example of the social act follows :

Gesture: A friend waves to me from across the street.

Perception: I may interpret this as a friendly greeting on his/her part. Or, since we had a violent argument only this morning, I perceive it as sarcastic.

Manipulation: I wave back. Or, if I view the wave as sarcastic, I may not wave back, but look in the other direction.

Consummation: We continue our separate ways. And the act ends. But does it? The essence of social behavior, according to Mead, is found in the fact that the meaning in any social act is not inherent in the act itself, but is governed by the response of the other person. The original gesture (a stimulus) did not determine what would happen (a response). Rather, it established a plan of action, a blue-print of what was likely to occur in the future. When I wave back, this gives one meaning to the act. If, however, I refuse to wave back, the act does not end by my refusal to 'respond' with some overt behavior. In terms of the cultural expectations that both my friend and myself share, we understand in our perception of the overt behavior that my refusal to wave under those conditions gives to the act a very different meaning than if I had responded with a wave.

To refuse to return a greeting charges the act with a high level of emotional meaning, perhaps even more so than the automatic return of a wave as an automatic response. The cumulative nature of behavior means that the latter response may serve as a stimulus to the other individual and help to determine the nature of his response to me the next time we encounter one another (see especially Mead, 1910b:174–80). All of the early interactionists insisted that human behavior is accumulative and does not occur in isolated bits and pieces with no reference to the past or future happenings of our lives. It is cumulative and constructive; i.e. our acts, responses, and perceptions are continually built upon those that are present in our social reper-tory at any one time. Behavior, as Cooley said of society, is tied together through a vast web of social behavior, mental constructions, and shared expectations. Gestures always have reference to the future (Lee, 1945:14):

> The teleological or functional nature of the act implies its division into various stages, logically and temporally related. A purposive activity implies a qualitative change of state as the activity pro-ceeds, e.g. from a hungry to a satisfied being. Each state has a value in terms of the function as a whole, according to the extent to which the end is realized in it. A function begins in want or a feeling of incompletion and ends in satisfaction, or a feeling of completion. In between these two feelings is another feeling; that of interest.

The basis of the relationship between the individual and society rests in the idea of mutual dependence that is implicit in the social act. What the environment provides in the sense of meaningful condi-tions for the direction of the act depends upon the selectivity of the organism. A 'thing' becomes recognizable as a social object through perception of its potentialities as an element in the selectivity process. In other words, it becomes defined in terms of function—which leads

Troyer (1946:201) to define objects as 'collapsed acts'—signs of what would happen if certain forms of behavior were carried to completion. At the personal level, the completion of the social act indicates the processes that make human society possible. Mead writes (1938: 137):

> The very stimulus which one gives to another to carry out his part of the common act affects the individual who so affects the other in the same sense. He tends to arouse the activity in himself which he arouses in the other. He also can in some degree so place himself in the place of the other or the places of others that he can share their experience. Thus, the varied means which belong to complicated human society can in varying degrees enter into the experience of many members, and the relationship between the means and the end can enter the experience of the individual.

The phylogenetic distinction between human societies and the lower forms of animal life is based upon the fact that, at the human level, society is largely dependent upon a social differentiation that takes the place of the physiological differentiations of the insects and lower forms of animal life—where the individual ends expand through communication and participation, which provide the content of human society (Mead, 1938:137). For Mead, then, social conduct becomes that which is mediated by the stimulations of others, which lead to responses which again affect these other forms (1912b:401). Society represents the macrocosm of all those processes involved in thought, perception, and the interaction of two individuals (1917:592–3):

> We must recognize that the most concrete and most fully realized society is not that which is represented in institutions as such, but that which is found in the interplay of social habits and customs, in the readjustment of personal interests that have come into conflict and which take place outside of court, in the change of social attitude that is not dependent upon an act of legislation. . . . Though human attitudes are far older than human institutions and seem to retain identities of structure that make us at home in the heart of every man whose story has come down to us from the written and unwritten past, yet these attitudes take on new forms as they gather new social content.

As did Dewey, Mead dissociated himself from the earlier sociological views of language. L. Ward, the father of American sociology, for example, had believed that language in humans was the natural result of being born human. Men and women began to speak as a natural condition of part of the fact of being human, and the association between vocal gestures and objects which they signified was made simple through an inborn rationalizing process that was also common to the species. Mead, on the other hand, wrote that language (1932:167):

> arises out of co-operative activities, such as those involved in sex, parenthood, fighting, herding, and the like, in which some phase of the act of one form . . . acts as a stimulus to others to carry on their parts of the social acts.

Language is anything but an individual experience, and the rules that govern its usage in any society cannot be understood with reference to particular individuals (1904:377). Vocal gestures and the behavior that is linked to them in human societies provide the basis for symbolic interaction. Vocal gestures in the form of symbols are (1934:181):

> nothing but a stimulus whose response is given in advance. That is all we mean by a symbol. There is a word and a blow. The blow is the historical antecedent of the word, but if the word means an insult, the response is one now involved in the word, something given in the very stimulus itself. That is all that is meant by a symbol.

Reasoning power in human beings, as manifested in their individual and social behavior, involves references to the relationships between things by the use of the symbols that are learned through interaction in a particular society. 'No individual . . . which has not come into the use of such symbols is rational. A system of these symbols is . . . language' (1938:518). Because of the universal nature of the symbol systems that are used in any society, Mead believed that language becomes the principal vehicle for social control (see also Lee, 1945: 10).

At one with the other pragmatists, Mead was concerned about the future development of American society, and was rather optimistic regarding the potentialities of society. Here, Mead wrote, one found (1930:104):

> freedom within certain rather rigid but very wide boundaries, to work out immediate politics and business with no reverential sense

of a pre-existing social order within which they must take their place and whose values they must preserve . . . individualism, perhaps uncouth, but unafraid.

The establishment of social control and cooperation, which is necessary for the survival of society, depends upon the degree to which individuals in society are able to assume the attitudes of the others who are involved with them in a common endeavor (see especially Mead, 1924; Petras, 1968a). The way in which this is to come about in human society is explained by Mead within the framework of the philosophy of the present, and this becomes the subject for his theory of self-emergence.

We have already indicated the close philosophical relationship between Dewey and Mead. The concern for social and educational reform which was so evident in the early works of Mead, already discussed here, diminished over time. With Dewey, however, the opposite effect can be observed. Both, however, shared the pragmatist's concern with the need for a changing system of ethics and values that would be based upon the reality of a changing society. While all of the pragmatists, especially James, were intrigued with the idea of time and the role that the temporal factor played in social behavior, it was not the subject of as much attention from them as it received in the works of Mead. It is Mead's philosophy of the present which allows him to establish the principle that human beings, through their simultaneous existence in two systems of social reality, act as both determined and determiners.

In Mead's view, persons both control and are controlled simultaneously by their environments. The pragmatic view of time has been examined by Tremmel, who writes (1957:7):

Change is not conceived of as necessarily progressive and orderly, but may be complete change, discontinuous and absolutely radical. Change so conceived brings with it the concomitant category of *novelty*. If change is complete, then newness is also complete. In pragmatism an event may possess structural characteristics which are absolutely novel. . . . In its basic categories, pragmatism rejects the ancient principle that nothing can come from nothing. No other world theory asserts change and novelty in so radical a sense.

Time is to be conceptualized in terms of change. And, time is defined as the duration of a particular event. Thus, time is a qualitative, and not quantitative, phenomenon present in the universe. Quantitative time, e.g. hours, days, years, need not have any reference to the fact that time itself may vary in response to the duration of a particular event and our perception of it. Two events taking place within the period of 'one hour' may vary in time, for the times *does* move more slowly during a bad time and the times *does* move more rapidly during a good time. Mead's theory was developed only several months before his death and was the subject of a series of lectures. These have been published as *The Philosophy of the Present* (1932: 28–9):

> The question arises whether the past arising in memory and in the projection of this still further backwards, refers to events which existed as such continuous presents passing into each other, or to that conditioning phase of the passing present which enables us to determine conduct with reference to the future which is also arising in the present. It is this latter thesis which I am maintaining.

The past is not a fixed condition of a structured time period, but may vary in accordance with any particular present (1932 : 31):

> If we had every possible document and every possible monument from the period of J. Caesar we should unquestionably have a truer picture of the man and of what occurred in his lifetime, but it would be a truth which belongs to this present, and a later present would reconstruct it from the standpoint of its own emergent nature.

The implications and relevance of this theory regarding the role of time in human and social behavior has been summarized by Tonness, who writes (1932 : 601):

> Reality is found in the natural process. The forms of this process, that is, the point at which nature displays its processional character, is the happening events where characters emerge and active existences continue or break. This field of emergent events is the present; the structure of the present is the emergent events, and this structure is basic to time itself. Thus, by this definition, the present becomes the seat of reality. Now, if reality is identified with the process of nature, and if the actuality of this process is in the active and emergent happenings, and if these happenings define the scope of the present, then, of necessity, that which is

not in the present because it is not a happening, because it is not in the actuality of the process, must fall outside of the field of reality. The former stage of the now on-going process is no longer in activity; it has ceased to exist as process. To say that the former stage is left behind or is past means that its reality ceased when the happenings of that stage expired. The metaphysical reality of the past, therefore, must be denied.

As Murphy has pointed out, the past may, in this view, be seen as both novel and irrevocable. That is, each definite present has its own irrevocable past, but the past is novel for each present (Murphy, 1932 : xviii).

Mead states that 'the world that comes to us from the past possesses and controls us. We possess and control the world that we discover and invent. . . . This is the world of the moral order' (1923 : 247). Mead's identification of reality as being situated within emergent process is further exemplified with his insistence that an animal is both creatively alive and a part of a shared phylogenetic world. Because of this, life is an emergent and extends its influence to the environment around it. 'It is because the conscious individual is both an animal and is also able to look before and after that consciousness emerges with the meanings and values with which it informs the world' (1932 : 66). This fact of the individual existing in 'dual systems' was expressed by Mead through the concept of sociality. Lee writes (1945 : 9):

If we define sociality as the presence of a reality in two systems, we see that the individual is social. He belongs to a system which determines him in part, and at the same time to a system which he determines [see also Pfeutze, 1954].

Men and woman share a dual existence in the sense that all are part of both the phylogenetic and irrevocable past world, as well as a social order which antedates their existence as necessary for individuals to develop into *human* beings (1938 : 153):

I wish to emphasize . . . : the appearance of the self is antedated by the tendencies to take the attitudes of the others, so that the existence of the others is not a reflection of his self-experiences into other individuals. The others are not relative to his self, but his self and the others are relative to the perspective of his self organism.

As consciousness of others precedes consciousness of self, so too does social consciousness precede physical consciousness (Bittner, 1931). 'Experience in its original form became reflective in the recognition of selves, and only gradually was there differentiated a reflective experience of things which were purely physical' (Mead, 1910b : 180). And, processes of thought and communication are possible only on the presupposition of a social process (1934 : 260). 'The others and the self arise in the social act together. The context of the act may be said to lie within the organism but it is projected into the other only in the sense in which it is projected into the self . . .' (1932 : 169). While this emphasis upon the importance of social factors in the individual-and-society relationship is common in social psychology today, it is well to remember that (Tremmel, 1957 : 12):

> In this kind of thinking Mead is an innovator. . . . The thinkers who preceded him generally conceived of society as a group of interrelated individuals. Mead everywhere insists on the primacy of society. An individual is merely an abstraction from a social group.

The self development processes in children were characterized by Mead in two general stages, each of which had been implicitly discussed in the early literature on educational reform. Play is characterized by spontaneity on the part of the child—non-determinacy. Its importance rests with the part it plays in enabling the development of elementary role-taking. Game, on the other hand, results from an internalization of the roles of others. In this sense game represents a shift from a non-determinate system to a determined one. In the first process the individual self is constituted simply by an organization of the particular attitudes of other individuals towards himself/herself and towards one another in the specific social acts in which he or she participates with them (see Mead, 1934 : 158). Without the process labeled 'game' (1932 : 85):

> The animal could never reach the goal of becoming an object to himself as a whole until it could enter into a larger system within which it could play various roles. . . . It is this development that a society whose life process is mediated by communication has made possible. It is here that mental life arises—with this continual passing from one system to another, with the occupation of both in passage and with the systematic structures that each involves. It is the realm of continual emergence.

The self becomes individually incorporated (1932 : 375):

> through . . . having assumed the generalized attitude of a member
> of the group to which the self belongs, a group that widens until
> it takes in all rational individuals, that is all individuals who could
> indicate to one another universal characters and objects in co-opera-
> tive activity [see also Mead, 1917].

The self is comprised of two component processes, the I and the
Me, which represent internalized dual systems of non-determinacy
and determinacy. Since life is part of an emergent process, the growth
of the self arises out of a partial disintegration—the appearance of
the different interests, the reconstruction of the social world, and the
consequent appearances of a new self that answers to new objects
(Bittner, 1931 : 11). As Mead (1912b : 405) asserts:

> The 'I' or the ego is identical with the analytic or synthetic pro-
> cesses of cognition, which in conflicting situations reconstructs
> out of the 'protoplasmic' states of consciousness both the empirical
> self (the 'me') and the world of object. The objective world is a
> mental construct and is defined in terms of the needs of the 'I' or
> the ego. It is a man's reply to his own talk. Such a me is not then
> an early formation which is then projected and ejected into the
> bodies of other people to give them the breath of human life. It
> is rather an importation from the field of social objects into an
> amorphous, unorganized field of what we call inner experience.
> Through the organization of this object, the self, this material is
> itself organized and brought under the control of the individual in
> the form of so-called self consciousness.

In conclusion, Mead's theory of human behavior offers more than a
theory of self development. Mead developed a theory which he considered to be congruent with universal phylogenetic processes and the
obvious facts of social life. The primary function of Mead's philosophy was to provide a context within which the nature of self was
bounded by time, as well as by space. The role of the future, in addition to the past, was recognized as an important variable in the motivation of behavior. With this idea, Mead added to the pragmatic
notion that motivational elements are dependent upon societal as
well as individual variables. For Mead, the role played by the individual was one of interpreting data furnished him or her in the
social situation. Thus, while the blocked impulses were satisfied

according to the individual's own desires, choices of potential solutions were bounded by the given facts of his or her presence in the larger network of society. The presence in two systems made men and women both determined and determiners.

DEFINING CHARACTERISTICS OF EARLY INTERACTIONISM

The previous discussions of the most significant individuals involved with the development of symbolic interactionism in American sociology have attempted to demonstrate two facts regarding the purpose of this work. First of all, they have been discussed in order to demonstrate the essentially individualistic orientation of early American sociology with respect to the ways in which the motivation of behavior was perceived (see especially Petras, 1970b; Schwendinger and Schwendinger, 1971). Secondly, we have attempted to point out how the individuals who played important roles in the development of interactionism differed with respect to the ways in which they defined social and human motivation. Now we shall consider their contributions collectively, in order to understand the original statement of what was considered to be symbolic interaction theory.

We have already pointed to several characteristics of the works of the thinkers we have discussed. On the one hand, there was a concern with the role of group factors as important elements for understanding behavior. Individuals in human society were not seen as units that are motivated by external or internal forces beyond their control, or within the confines of a more or less fixed structure. Rather, they were viewed as reflective or interacting units which comprise the societal entity. As Blumer (1953) has noted, it was viewed as nothing less than a point of logical necessity that the study of human behavior begin with the fact of human associations in society. While such a conceptualization has been common for several decades in American sociology, in 1928 it was characteristic only of the 'newer' sociology, which sought (Eubank, 1927:422):

> to make the group the focal center and to build up from its discoveries in concrete situations, a knowledge of the whole. In particular, this newer approach stresses intensive examination of interactions that take place within the group.

This, then, was a radically different position from that advocated by L. Ward and his students during the first years of American sociology.

These sociologists had advocated a view of the individual-and-society relationship that varied little from the position of the contract theorists. They believed that language and the potentialities of human communication were to be traced to the unique individuals, and these qualities were to be understood as characteristic of the species, with minimal reference to the fact of human association in groups. The conception of the relationship between the individual and society was one in which the social element was seen as evolving from the individual component. With regard to actual behavior, this conceptualization was reflected in an individualistic approach to such matters as social problems and motivation. The opposition to this conceptualization, which was presented in the works of James, Dewey, Cooley, Mead, and the later Thomas, took varying specific forms and was modified during their own careers; but, all converged with respect to a reconceptualization of the individual-and-society relationship. Within the setting of early American sociology, the notion of interaction and unity between the individual and society could be expressed only through an emphasis upon the role of the group (see especially Petras, 1966).

Dewey's training and background in both philosophy and psychology played an important role in the ways in which he developed his view of the importance of group factors. From his studies in psychology, he was gradually led to the conclusion that the interaction between the individual and his/her social situations provided the key for the understanding of behavior. He was, for this reason, able to conceive the nature of human behavior in terms of a circularity of interaction between the individual and the social group. As we have demonstrated earlier, Dewey's own thought can be characterized with reference to the movement of concern from instinct to the habit complex. By coupling his concerns in psychology with those of social reform and ethics, the pragmatic concerns, he established his theories at a level of analysis where they had direct relevance for sociology.

Dewey's attack upon the older view of the individual-and-society relationship struck at the core of early American sociology, which had, since the time of Ward, been closely identified with the notion of social reform and change. The shift in focus from the individual to the environment, which was advocated by Dewey, required a shift in the traditional locus of the 'causes' of social problems. In the new conceptualization, the conditions were considered to exist in the social environment. In other words, a new approach to the understanding of behavior was offered. If one wished to understand why an individual behaved in the manner that he/she did, one had to look to the social environment for the conditions of social interactions. This particular aspect of Dewey's theory can be directly traced to his concern for a reconstruction in philosophy. The reconstruction that he advocated was to be based upon the fact that social conditions vary over time as well as space, and this had to be taken into account when establishing ethical guide-lines for human behavior.

From the fields of psychology and philosophy, Dewey was led to an awareness of the importance of group factors in behavior. The influence of J. M. Baldwin and W. James cannot be disregarded. From Baldwin, Dewey received an appreciation of the nature of interaction between the individual and society. From James, he received influences which served to establish functional psychology in America. We would suggest that it was because of the interactional influence which they offered that Dewey never resorted to an explanation of behavior based entirely upon the role of social determinants and conditions. In summary, Dewey's reconceptualization of the individual and the group centered around the search for conditions that enter into human behavior in different societies at different times.

G. H. Mead, like Dewey, was led to an appreciation of the role of the group in human behavior through his involvement in the development of functional psychology. In the study of the mind, for example, emphasis was shifted from a physical structure to the mind's manifestations in behavior. Behavior, then, was reconceptualized as having its conditions in the social environment, not the structure of the human brain or body. Mead offered still another dimension to the growing awareness of the role of the group. As has been demonstrated, his writings show a noticeable eventual decline of interest in social reform and reconstruction. The direction of his psychology was established with the concern for self and personality development in human society. Because of this, his conceptualization of the group tended to be in terms of its representing an 'other.'

There are several implications regarding this type of conceptualization. First of all, the interpretive element is introduced into behavior at the human level. The individual's interpretation of the stimulus and the consequent effect that this had upon behavior had been considered by Dewey (1896) in his article, 'The Reflex Arc Concept in Psychology.' However, at the societal level, Dewey did not concern himself with the individual's interpretations of certain conditions, but with the very existence of the conditions themselves. For example, his concern with the elimination of social problems and with educational reform emphasized the *creation of certain conditions* which would establish a favorable environment in which the individual would act. This type of approach can also be seen in the early articles by Mead, especially as regards the establishment of favorable classroom situations for the development of learning. But, the emphasis changed as Mead developed more and more concern with the genesis and development of the self in humans.

Whereas it is possible to give a limited interpretation to the motivation of human behavior without reference to the individual's interpretation of the social conditions that are present, no valid explanation for the genesis of the 'social self' is possible with this limited approach. To develop a self requires a process whereby the individual person is able to incorporate the other into his/her own mind in order that the individual can learn to act towards himself/herself as toward others. This explains, in part, why Mead, in comparison with Dewey, devoted much of his time to the problem and processes of communication. It is through communication with the other that the self arises. Furthermore, it is not simply a matter of taking in the communication, but one of interpreting the intended meaning. The group, therefore, is conceived as a body of meanings which are the products of interacting individuals. Through a sharing of the meanings that develop in interaction, the individual and the group become part of a larger system, and both become, in the words of Cooley, two sides of the same coin. Rather than being simply a present condition in behavior, the group becomes a referent, a symbolic bond in the individual–society relationship.

Another implication arising from Mead's concern with the development of the self is the notion of emergence. As already pointed out, the idea of the reality of the present was used in a different sense, later on, by W. I. Thomas in his concept of the definition of the situation. The application of the notion of emergence from the realm of philosophy to that of the behavioral sciences had a significant effect upon the reconceptualization of the individual-and-society relationship. Essentially, it served to rule out a theory of extreme determinism by either groups or individual characters. Behavior was seen as having its focal point in the realm of an emergent present; and, therefore, a view was offered which presented a radical departure from the earlier writings of sociologists. Instinct theories of motivation had, more or less, ruled out any study of the individual's situation as necessary for the understanding of human behavior. Indeed, as long as the individual was seen as belonging to one more or less undifferentiated group, the situational aspect of human behavior was held to be inconsequential. But once the individual is viewed as reconstructing the past in terms of his/her present social situations and is seen as actively interpreting these past conditions so that they affect his or her future behavior, a theory based upon the individual-generated perspective, such as that of instinct theory, can no longer apply.

In a certain sense, the work of C. H. Cooley is closer to that of Dewey than Mead or, for that matter, Thomas. Dewey was concerned with the conditions in the social order that were necessary for a complete understanding of behavior. Cooley was interested in the same problem, and this interest took the form of a structural sociology which revolutionized the discipline. By differentiating the concept of the group into the dimensions of primary and secondary forms, Cooley accomplished two things. On the one hand, he offered a theory as to where one should look in order to find the most important conditions as far as the social motivation of the individual's behavior was concerned. Secondly, Cooley developed a methodology which could, at least, attempt to get at the more important social conditions affecting the individual's behavior. Studies of the life situation of the individual in relationship to the several forms of groups which could be delineated now became methodologically manageable.

Cooley's emphasis upon social processes, as well as his sociology of structure, provides an excellent example of the nature of the reconceptualization of the individual–society relationship proposed by the early interactionists. For the first time, the individual and society were seen as 'over-lapping' units. The older, individualistic psychology, which the interactionists had reacted against, characterized the thought of the early American sociologists. In the older individualism, the relationship was one of tension. For the most part, the maladjustments of individuals in the social order were traced to an unnatural suppression of the inherent tendencies of men and women. It was as if the individual and society were two separate and discrete units with opposing needs. Each was considered to be independent of the other, and each had an inherent tendency towards action which was diametrically opposed to the other. The conceptualization of human society in an organic framework was not an innovation by the early interactionists. The idea had previously been popularized by H. Spencer and his followers, who became leading targets of attacks by the interactionists. The difference between the two formulations rested in the nature of the perceived organic structure.

In the older formulation, individuals were considered to be engulfed by the organism of society in such a way as to preclude the individual injection of creativity into the social order. As we have seen, it was with reference to this point that W. James took issue with these ideas. It is easy to see how this early view of society, even though organic in nature, fostered an individualistic conception of the individual–society relationship. In part, the difficulty can be traced to the idea that the organic nature of society was a replication of the biological organism. Thus, individuals were conceived to be caught up in a network of forces over which they had no control, and in reality, the formulation turned out to be a 'false organicism.' Although the concept of the organism was present in the structural sense, the idea of an organic process characterized by the interaction between the individual units was lacking.

The new formulation, however, was conceived of in terms of what Eubank had called the 'new psychology,' not a biological framework. Immediate emphasis, therefore, was directed towards interaction processes, not structure. The significance of the development of functional psychology in the USA under the leadership of W. James and J. Dewey is clearly evident, as we have seen, in the works of the early interactionists. The concept of group was elevated to a new position by taking it out of an individualistic framework and placing it into a functional, interacting one.

The idea that the group had to be considered an important factor in the motivation of human behavior, therefore, arrived relatively late in the development of American sociology. As indicated, the tradition of instinct theories of motivation was most characteristic of the mainstream of early American sociology. Out of the tradition of James and Baldwin, however, developed the idea that the individual could be influenced by the social groups of which he/she was a member. James discussed this phenomenon along the lines of a social self—the idea that an individual would think of himself/herself in as many different ways as there were groups to which he or she belonged. Baldwin approached it through his work on the development of the self and personality in the child. Both of these individuals influenced the later thinking of Dewey, Cooley, and Mead, who, in turn, were indirectly influential upon the work of W. I. Thomas.

For these individuals, the group concept involved two significant ideas. First of all, the group was of an organic nature in the sense that it was composed of interacting individuals who shared certain ideas which defined their membership within the group. Secondly, the group provided the conditions for behavior by presenting shared meanings to each individual for his/her interpretation.

The particular manner in which these individuals reconceptualized the individual-and-society relationship by their emphasis upon the role of the group leads directly into the second major defining characteristic of early symbolic interactionism. This characteristic is a concern with the development of self and personality and the recognition that the biological factor in human beings cannot be ignored and must be dealt with in a satisfactory manner by any valid theory of motivation.

It is of particular interest to note that the early interactionists gave some recognition to the biological factors in behavior; but they were also among the schools most influential in bringing about the decline and fall of instinct theories of motivation within the discipline. Thus, they recognized that the social group alone could not account for a complete understanding of human and social behavior. There is always an interaction process, that has to be fully explored, between the innate impulses of the human organism and the social forces. We shall now look a little more closely at the differences in the two conceptions, 'instinct' and 'impulse.'

With respect to the basic elements involved in the motivation of human behavior, the early American sociologists had been quite explicit. The causes were to be found within the individual. Ward, for example, traced the motivation of behavior to innate tendencies which were then manifested in behavior through the 'natural' fear of pain and the desire to seek after pleasure. For the most part, the role played by the group in this process was to hinder nature. In other words, the older psychology, which stressed the dualism between the individual and society, was nicely coupled with instinct theories of motivation. The impulse—as opposed to instinct—differs in that its satisfaction can take place only within the bounds of what is called human society. As used by the early interactionists, the term 'impulse' was conceived as possessing a major defining characteristic of undifferentiated activity. Nothing specific was given in the behavior itself in order to assure a particular type of end for satisfaction. The result was a unique theory, combining the biological and the social nature of human beings, in which the innate tendencies, in the form of undifferentiated activity, had their ends defined by culture. Membership in a social group was predicated as a prerequisite for the realization of the biological potential, for this is the only way that the undifferentiated activities can take on meaning for oneself and other members of society.

Without any doubt, it was W. I. Thomas who provided the greatest degree of popularization for the notion of the impulse in American sociology. The concept of the wish was, in actuality, an attempt to operationalize the combining of the biological and social natures of humans, which had previously been restricted more or less to the theoretical level. Of equal significance is the fact that Thomas was one of the first thinkers to extend the principles of symbolic interaction theory, developed with reference to the self and personality in the child, to the adult level of life. The importance of this fact resides in the fact that it was the first major instance of a demonstration of the relevancy of the symbolic interactionist approach to behavior for the everyday world of taken-for-granted activity. In the same fashion, the concepts of value and attitude can be seen as an attempt to operationalize the nature of the individual–society relationship to a level where empirical studies would be possible. According to Thomas, this relationship is bounded by activity—a view that provides an excellent example of the reconceptualization of the relationship in terms of process rather than structure. None of the early interactionists was able to state as clearly as Thomas the fact that the individual must continually redefine his position relative to the social groups of which he is a member. Again, a significant element in this view was Thomas' extension of self and personality theory to the adult level. Establishment of the principle that attitudes and values change only in relationship to one another clarified the interactionist view of both the unity of the individual and society and the organic nature of the relationship.

The third defining characteristic of early interactionism lies in the meaning of the term 'symbolic behavior.' It is common in American sociology today to find the term 'language' used as synonymous with the symbolic element. This usage has tended to contribute to the mistaken belief that language, to the exclusion of other forms of communication, played the most important role as the symbolic element in the early interactionists' theories. But actually, it was only with reference to certain specific aspects of the theory that language was elevated to a primary position in the symbolic element, e.g. Mead on self reflexiveness. Important aspects of this element were included in the notion of communication by means of non-vocal gestures among individuals who are members of the same social order. As the boundaries of the group were delimited through the mental constructs held by its members, the symbolic element was defined in terms of the institutions, norms, and values as interpreted by the individual, who then had to draw upon these shared meanings when making his/her own interpretations. The important point emphasized by the early interactionists was the means by which human beings communicated. While this idea may seem little more than common sense today, it represented, as we have seen, a distinct departure from the earlier sociological tradition. The earlier conception of society was that of an aggregation of individuals held together through physical limitations. The symbolic interactionists developed the conception of society as held together by shared meanings. It is here that we find the significance of the symbolic element. This conception allowed for the differentiation of the physical definition of society into several smaller groups, each with a different degree of influence depending upon the position it occupied in the individual's hierarchy of mental constructs. This is what Cooley had emphasized in the mental constructs of the primary group, not the physical characteristics. It followed, therefore, that as a more differentiated concept of the social group developed, the units of motivation were recognized to exist at several different levels outside of the human organism. In Dewey's terminology, the field of potential stimuli to be utilized by the individual was not only increased but also given a preference order in terms of the role each was likely to play in influencing the individual's behavior. With the concept of the situation, Thomas provided a further differentiation by re-introducing the temporal factor, which had played a role in the theories of Mead. Unlike the primary group, the situation could not be structurally defined. As noted earlier, Dewey devoted most of his attention to the conditions in the social order when speaking of interaction at the societal level. On the other hand, Thomas stressed the *interpretation* of these conditions in his theory of behavior. Influences from the traditional primary groups that were important during the individual's life were held to be relevant to his/her behavior only if they were interpreted as being meaningful with reference to an immediate situation. This was a dimension of behavior that had not been dealt with by Cooley and could, in part, account for the concern he exhibited over the lack of primary-type groups for adults in a complex and rapidly changing society. Indeed, it is curious as to why Cooley, who up to that time had formulated the most complete theory of the group as both an organism and a mental construct, all but neglected the interpretive element in behavior.

A final defining characteristic of early symbolic interactionism is found in the nature of the research that it generated in American sociology. Its primary influence upon early research came from two directions. First of all, the notion of interaction as a crucial link between the individual and the social group became a subject of concern in several areas. Secondly, a more direct influence could be noted in the adoption of the method of sympathetic introspection, best exemplified at that time with the publication of *The Polish Peasant in Europe and America* (Thomas and Znaniecki, 1918).

With respect to these two characteristics, it is necessary, at least, to mention the influence of the early textbook by Park and Burgess, *Introduction to the Science of Sociology* (1921). In his overview of the development of American sociology, R. E. L. Faris writes (1964: 27–8):

> No other book had done so much to standardize the content of sociology. Ward's 'science of sciences' was omitted, philosophy of history was turned back to historians, humanitarian concerns with poverty and related afflictions were located out toward the boundaries of the field. . . . Park and Burgess sensed the promise in investigations of social processes, in interaction (social psychology), and in the nature of organization.

In their preface, Park and Burgess had written (1921 : vii):

> The editors desire to express their indebtedness to Dr. W. I. Thomas for the point of view and scheme of organization of materials which have been largely adopted in this book.

It would not be correct, however, to say that the only source of the perspective they adopted came from the Chicago school of early symbolic interactionism. The fact that Park had studied with G. Simmel is quite evident, and a major part of the interaction influence must be traced to this period in the development of Park's thought.

Although the book was published several years before most American sociologists were to gain even an elementary appreciation of Simmel's theories, he is the most frequently cited figure in the more than one thousand pages of text. The book, therefore, did much to foster an independent development of the concern for interaction in American sociology. In 1926, E. E. Eubank published a study which traced the development of the concepts of 'group,' 'situation,' and 'interaction' in American sociology. Concentrating upon the 'most authoritative voices' in the American Sociological Society, he analyzed seven textbooks and came to the conclusion that *Introduction to the Science of Sociology* was the only one to combine the concepts of group and interaction. As we have seen, these were the key concepts of early symbolic interactionism.

The historical significance of the rise of symbolic interactionism in American sociology has been all but forgotten today. Few sociologists recognize the role this theory played in the development and establishment of the concept of 'group' in the discipline and the decline of theories based upon an individual-generated perspective. Its success along these lines can be measured by the paucity of attention directed towards these aspects of the theory today. Thus, today, no one questions either the importance of the group as a factor in the motivation of behavior or that the sources of motivation do not reside in instincts. What one finds, instead, is that the vast majority of the later attempts to test aspects of the theory have dealt with the concepts of 'self,' 'identity,' and 'role.' Three intervening developments have created a resurgence of interest in the theory.

First of all, an increase in interest in self psychology and the concept of identity has occurred. Secondly, in the past twenty years especially, we have witnessed the development of role theory. Finally, the rise of the concept 'reference group' has stimulated a growing body of research. As far as American sociology is concerned, it was the early formulation of interactionism which provided the basis for each of these subsequent developments. The resurgence of symbolic interactionism in the past five years, however, may be more directly traceable to the development of ethnomethodology and dramaturgical sociology. These developments will be treated in a later section of this work.

chapter 2

Varieties of symbolic interactionism

INTRODUCTORY REMARKS

Contemporary symbolic interactionism comprehends, as we have indicated, several diverse schools of thought. Their number and character vary according to differing conceptions of the central ideas that constitute the general orientation. As few as only two schools have been distinguished by some commentators, and as many as ten by one commentator.

Meltzer and Petras (1970; also see Manis and Meltzer, 1967, 1972), for example, describe two major varieties, the Chicago and Iowa schools, on the basis, primarily, of differences in preferred methodology. 'Conventional' and 'unconventional' varieties, as identified chiefly by varying definitions of key concepts, are designated by Vaughan and Reynolds (1968). Refining the distinctions made in the foregoing studies, Reynolds and Meltzer (1973) distinguish three methodologically distinct groups of interactionists: an 'unorthodox' group (favoring participant observation), a 'semi-conventional' group (favoring positivism), and a 'conventional' group (favoring a combination of methods).

Other commentators have broadened the range of variants within symbolic interactionism. An anthology of papers on ethnomethodology designates its topic as one of several approaches 'derived from' symbolic interactionism (Dreitzel, 1970). Other such approaches, according to the editor, are the 'phenomenological theorizing' of P. Berger and T. Luckmann in their book on *The Social Construction of Reality* (1967), 'philosophical anthropology,' and the work of E. Goffman. All of these approaches emphasize the meaning element in everyday activities. Similarly, one influential chronicler of recent developments in symbolic interaction theory lists as 'sub- or related orientations' such approaches as role theory, reference group theory, the social perception and person perception viewpoint, the dramaturgical school, the interpersonal theory of psychiatry proposed by H. S. Sullivan, the Sapir-Whorf-Cassirer language and culture orientation, phenomenological theory, self theory, and others (Kuhn, 1964). These 'offshoots' of interactionism are held to have stemmed from the essential ambiguities and contradictions in the Meadian statement of the general theory, particularly with regard to the issue of determinacy and indeterminacy in human conduct. And, finally, Warshay (1971) identifies the following varieties:

> (1) the Blumer school, emphasizing the more subjective aspects . . . ; (2) the Iowa school, stressing self-theory and a positivistic methodology . . . ; (3) an emphasis on interaction with de-emphasis on language . . .; (4) a role-theory view with a cognitive emphasis within a moderate scientific tradition . . . ; (5) the 'dramaturgical' school, featuring the intricacies of role and self manipulation . . . ; (6) a field-theory version combining Mead, Lewin, and Lundberg . . . ; (7) an existential brand; (8) ethnomethodology, stressing the complexity and fluidity of the web of social life with a humanist-participatory methodology.

Out of the welter of 'schools' indicated in the foregoing paragraphs, we have selected four for discussion. These four—the Chicago school, the Iowa school, the dramaturgical approach, and ethnomethodology—appear to be clearly distinct orientations within symbolic interactionism. More distinctly than the many other listed varieties, each adopts a perspective that includes basic constituent elements of the larger framework while, simultaneously, adding or subtracting other elements of a less basic character.

Common to the four varieties are the basic premises of symbolic interactionism described by Blumer, which have been presented on the first page of this book. To repeat them: (1) human beings act toward things on the basis of the meanings that the things have for them; (2) these meanings are a product of social interaction in human society; and (3) these meanings are modified and handled through an interpretive process that is used by each person in dealing with the things he/she encounters. In summary, we can say that, as varieties of symbolic interactionism, all of these orientations share the substantive view that human beings construct their realities in a process of interaction with other human beings. As a corollary, each orientation accepts, to some degree, the methodological necessity of 'getting inside' the reality of the actor in an effort to understand this reality as the actor does.

In examining the selected orientations, we shall focus attention primarily upon the ideas of one major exponent, or exemplar, of each orientation. To do otherwise would entail a loss of coherence, for a wider coverage would require the inclusion of numerous minor qualifications and reservations. Because they represent the two most contrastive varieties, the Chicago and Iowa schools will be treated together, in point-counterpoint fashion. The dramaturgical school and ethnomethodology will receive separate treatments. Our discussion of each variety will assume at least a passing familiarity on the part of the reader.

THE CHICAGO AND IOWA SCHOOLS[1]

During the major portion of the past generation, the two leading progenitors of the symbolic interactionist perspective have been H. G. Blumer and the late M. H. Kuhn. Through his writings and his students at the University of Chicago and the University of California (Berkeley), Blumer has elaborated the best-known variety of interactionism—an approach we call the Chicago school. This approach continues the classical, Meadian tradition. The Iowa school developed through the work of Kuhn and his students at the State University of Iowa. This orientation, sustained almost exclusively, until quite recently, by articles published in the *Sociological Quarterly*, represents a more eclectic form of interactionism. The two schools differ in important substantive and methodological matters, which can be delineated and illustrated from the writings of the chief progenitor of each school. These matters reflect broader controversies throughout the behavior disciplines.

Most influential of the interactionists we shall be considering, Blumer has had a career that requires only brief exposition here. His doctoral work at the University of Chicago brought him into close association with Mead and E. Faris (an early interactionist), as well as with R. E. Park (whose work in collective behavior Blumer later expounded). Beginning in 1925, three years prior to his receipt of the doctorate, he held a position in the Department of Sociology at Chicago, where he established himself as the inheritor of Mead's mantle in symbolic interactionism. In 1952 he joined the faculty of the Department at Berkeley.

A brief examination of Kuhn's intellectual background may assist an effort to understand his modifications of symbolic interactionism. While earning his Master's and Doctor's degrees at the University of Wisconsin, Kuhn studied with K. Young, an eclectic proponent of the Meadian perspective. Following brief periods in the faculties of the University of Wisconsin, Whittier College, and Mount Holyoke College, Kuhn established himself at the State University of Iowa in 1946, remaining there until his death in 1963. In this latter post, he taught graduate students who were also being exposed to the logical positivism of G. Bergman and to K. Spence's positivistic works in psychology and in the philosophy of science. That these briefly sketched currents of thought influenced Kuhn's work is readily apparent.

Before launching upon the differences between the Chicago and Iowa schools, we shall venture, briefly, to relate these schools to their respective social backgrounds. Taken as a general orientation, symbolic interactionism has been described as an almost predictable product of American society and culture. One writer comments (Shaskolsky, 1970:16):

> It is doubtful whether a theory such as symbolic interactionism could have arisen in any social and political context other than a society such as America's with its egalitarian ethos and its mobile class structure. The basic thesis on which it rests is clearly inapplicable to a class-structured society steeped in the formalistic, often fossilized, modes of behavior handed down from previous generations.

And more specifically (1970:20):

> symbolic interaction theory is a worthy attempt to create a unique philosophic rationale for the finer aspects of American society—for what is known at the more colloquial level as the American way of life, characterized as it is by respect for the individual and a belief in gradual change to meet society's fluctuating needs. Intrinsic to the theory is the sense of fluidity and its accent . . . on flexible interpersonal relationships as a basis for an understanding of the working of society.

While the foregoing comments may suggest the social sources of the general orientation, we must look elsewhere for clues to the differentiation of the Chicago and Iowa schools. In a series of pertinent articles, Reynolds offers empirical support for one plausible source (see Reynolds, *et al.*, 1970; Reynolds and McCart, 1972; Reynolds and Meltzer, 1973; Vaughan and Reynolds, 1968). It is his contention that certain associational patterns are conducive to the development and/or perpetuation of particular types of sociological work. Focusing upon patterns of institutional affiliation (fellow doctoral-level students, professors and students, and departmental colleagues), his studies indicate that representatives of the two schools exhibit different patterns. His data suggest that a relatively strong, multi-bonded network of supportive associations may account for the persistence of such unconventional approaches as the Chicago school's. On the other hand, the absence of a network of this kind may foster the development and persistence of an approach more harmonious with the prevailing perspectives in the discipline, as appears to be the case with the Iowa school.

It can be argued plausibly that the most fundamental point of divergence between the Chicago and Iowa schools is that of methodology. We find here, as in various disciplines studying human behavior, the opposition between 'humanistic' and 'scientific' viewpoints. Blumer argues the case for a distinctive methodology in the study of such behavior, while Kuhn stresses the unity of method in all scientific disciplines. Continuing the nineteenth-century distinction between *Geisteswissenschaften* and *Naturwissenschaften*, one position proposes an idiographic (or non-generalizing) function for behavioral studies, and the other a nomothetic (or generalizing) function. Thus, while Blumer strives simply 'to make modern society intelligible,' Kuhn seeks universal predictions of social conduct. Three intertwined topics represent the basic specifics of this methodological divergence: (1) the relative merits of phenomenological and operational approaches; (2) the appropriate techniques of observation; and (3) the nature of the concepts best suited for the analysis of human behavior.

Although both Blumer and Kuhn claim to be interested in what goes on 'inside the heads' of humans, their approaches to this subject-matter differ significantly. Blumer's advocacy of a special methodology lays heavy stress upon the need for insightfully 'feeling one's way inside the experience of the actor.' The student of human conduct, he contends, must get inside the actor's world and must see the world as the actor sees it, for the actor's behavior takes place on the basis of his/her own particular meanings. Through some form of sympathetic introspection, the student must take the standpoint of the acting unit (person or group) whose behavior he/she is studying and must attempt to use each actor's own categories in capturing that actor's world of meaning. This intuitive, *verstehende* approach emphasizes intimate understanding more than inter-subjective agreement among investigators.

In a posthumously published article, Kuhn (1964:72) describes as 'perhaps the most significant contribution of the Iowa research' its demonstration 'that the key ideas of symbolic interactionism could be operationalized and utilized successfully in empirical research.' Continuing in this vein, he refers to self theory (his designation of what we have labeled the 'Iowa school') as an effort to develop a set of generalizations tested by empirical research—in contrast with the earlier 'body of conjectural and deductive orientations' constituting symbolic interactionism. It is with this effort in mind that Kuhn sought to 'empiricize' Mead's ideas, reconceptualizing or abandoning those he deemed 'non-empirical' and developing observational techniques that were consistent with this aim. His writings repeatedly sounded the call for the operational definition of concepts, for methods that would meet 'the usual scientific criteria,' and for a 'standardized, objective, and dependable process of measurement . . . of significant variables' (Hickman and Kuhn, 1956:224-5). Kuhn and the Iowa school do not, however, reject the study of the covert aspects of human behavior. Rather, they urge the utilization of objective overt-behavioral indices (chiefly verbal protocols by the actor) of the covert aspects.

In the light of Blumer's insistence upon sympathetic introspection, it is entirely expectable that he advocates the use of such observational techniques as life histories, autobiographies, case studies, diaries, letters, interviews (especially of the free, or non-directive, type), and, most importantly, participant observation. Only through intimate association with those who are being studied, he maintains, can the investigator enter their inner worlds. His basic criticism of the experimental, instrumental, and quantitative methodology, in the form of questionnaires, schedules, tests, laboratory procedures, and detached observation 'from the outside,' is that they completely fail to catch the 'meanings' that crucially mediate, and determine how individuals respond to, objects and situations. Apparently untroubled by critics of the 'soft science' techniques, Blumer shrugs off such strictures against these techniques as the following: these techniques are subjective and, hence, unsuited to the development of scientific knowledge; information gathered through their use is too variable and unique for comparison and generalization; they tend to be too time-consuming for convenient use; it is not known how we can teach the subtle skills required in their use; and they do not, typically, lend themselves to the conventional testing of explicitly formulated theories by procedures subject to independent validation. Striking back against the methods that characterize mainstream American sociology, Blumer (1969: 26–7) writes:

> The overwhelming bulk of what passes today as methodology is made up of such preoccupations as the following: the devising and use of sophisticated research techniques, usually of advanced statistical character; the construction of logical and mathematical models, all too frequently guided by a criterion of elegance; the elaboration of formal schemes on how to construct concepts and theories; valiant application of imported schemes, such as input-output analysis, systems analysis, and stochastic analysis; studious conformity to the canons of research design; and the promotion of a particular procedure, such as survey research, as *the* method of scientific study. I marvel at the supreme confidence with which these preoccupations are advanced as the stuff of metholology.

A case can plausibly be made for equating Kuhn's methodology with the technique of the twenty statements test (TST), as C. Tucker (1966) does. Known also as the 'Who Am I?' test, the TST was developed by Kuhn, in 1950, as part of his endeavour to transform the concepts of symbolic interactionism into variables that might be employable in generating and testing empirical propositions. In his concern with the construction of an instrument for eliciting attributes of the self, Kuhn explicitly rejected as unfeasible all attempts to 'get inside the individual and observe these interior plans of action directly' or to infer them from overt behavior. He concluded, rather, that such devices as questionnaires and attitude scales could be adapted to identify and measure self-attributes. The resultant instrument, based upon an open-response model, requires a content analysis of the responses and can be subjected to Guttman-scale analysis. Today, the TST is the most widely used technique for studying self-conceptions, has had a section (entitled 'Iowa Studies in Self-Attitudes') devoted to it at the 1958 meetings of the American

Sociological Association, has been utilized in over 100 reported researches, and achieved a measure of national popular attention when it was administered to the early astronauts (Spitzer, *et al.*, no date).

To study 'the natural social world of our experience'—a phrase that recurs in his writings—Blumer urges the employment of 'sensitizing concepts.' As Sjoberg and Nett (1968:59) comment: 'That Blumer objects to operational definitions of concepts and advocates the use of "sensitizing concepts" is consistent with his image of social reality.' The image includes both societal fluidity and a humanistic view of the actor's ability to shape and reshape his/her environment. Contrasting conventional scientific concepts ('definitive concepts') with sensitizing concepts, Blumer asserts that the former provide prescriptions of what to see, while the latter merely suggest directions along which to look. A concept should, he adds, sensitize one to the task of 'working with and through the distinctive nature of the empirical instance, instead of casting the unique nature aside . . .' (Blumer, 1954:8). In Blumer's view, the student of human conduct moves from the abstract concept to the concrete distinctiveness of the instance; for, he/she must use the distinctive expression in order to discern the common. Putting it more fully:

> Because of the varying nature of the concrete expression from instance to instance we have to rely, apparently, on general guides and not on fixed objective traits or modes of expression. To invert the matter, since what we infer does not express itself in the same fixed way, we are not able to rely on fixed objective expressions to make the inference.

We can be quite brief in presenting the viewpoint of Kuhn and the Iowa school on the nature and function of concepts, for theirs is the conventional viewpoint within present-day sociology. In Kuhn's effort to convert the imprecise Meadian concepts into researchable 'variables,' he has formulated explicitly operational definitions of 'self,' 'social act,' 'social object,' 'reference group,' and other concepts. An instructive example is the following excerpt from his discussion of the self: 'Operationally the self may be defined . . . as answers which an individual gives to the question which he directs to himself, "Who am I?" or the question another directs to him, such as "What kind of a person are you?," "Who are you?" etc.' (no date: 4). These proposed questions, of course, are the basis of the TST.

A final issue in the methodological divergences between the two schools relates to Blumer's attack on the use in social inquiry of 'variables'—with their mechanistic implications of a static, stimulus-response image of human behavior. Despite Kuhn's rejection of psychological behaviorism, his quest for variables commits him to some of its favored methodological orientations, as we have already seen. Thus, it is evident that our two protagonists assign different priorities to relevant understanding versus precise analysis, as well as to the discovery of ideas versus the testing of propositional knowledge. We can plausibly argue, further, that Blumer's image of humans led him to a particular methodology, while Kuhn's methodological predilections led him to a particular image of humans. We now turn to these somewhat contrasting images.

A second salient difference between the two schools raises the ancient question of whether human behavior is free or determined. Conceiving such behavior in terms of an interplay between the spontaneous and the socially-derived aspects of the self, Blumer builds into the behavior an unpredictable, indeterminate dimension. For him, this interplay is the fundamental source of innovation in human society. By contrast, exponents of the Iowa school reject both indeterminism in human conduct and the explanation of social innovation in terms of the emergent, creative element in human acts. The key issue is the place of impulse in conduct.

In order to facilitate presentation of this issue, we shall briefly review certain ideas touched on in chapter 1 of this book. Following Mead's treatment quite closely, Blumer views the self as involving two analytically distinguishable phases, the I and the Me. The first of these analytical entities is the impulsive tendency of the individual. It is the initial, spontaneous, unorganized aspect of human experience. It represents, then, the undisciplined, unrestrained, and undirected tendencies of the individual, which take the form of diffuse and undifferentiated activity. An example would be one's immediate impulse of anger upon being struck by another. The Me, on the other hand, represents the incorporated other within the individual. Hence, it comprises the organized set of attitudes and definitions prevailing within the group. In any given situation, the Me constitutes the generalized other and, often, some particular other. Every act begins in the form of an I and, generally, ends in the form of a Me. For the I constitutes the initiation of the act prior to its coming under the control of the definitions or expectations of others (the Me). The I, thus, provides propulsion, while the Me provides direction, to the act. Human behavior, then, is viewed as an ongoing series of initiations of incipient acts by impulses (the I) and of guidance of the acts by the Me. The act is a resultant of this dialectical interplay and 'cannot be accounted for by factors which precede the act' (Blumer, 1962 : 183).

It is not entirely clear from Blumer's work whether the indeterminacy that characterizes human conduct is the product simply of the exploratory, improvising, and impulsive I or is a more complex emergent from the interaction between the I and the Me. Contrasting the symbolic-interactionist view with stimulus-response approaches and other conventional views, he points out that the former is interested in *action*, and the latter in *reaction*. More specifically, he contends that activity begins with an inner impulse rather than with an external stimulus, and that this activity may undergo a significant course of development before coming to overt expression. This development may bring the emergence of new definitions and new arrangements of definitions. In any case, Blumer expresses skepticism of social-scientific theories that purport to embody determinate, precisely predictive propositions.

In Kuhn's self theory we find no explicit cognizance of either impulses or the I and Me composition of the self. For him, as for conventional role theory, behavior is socially determined—by the actor's definitions, particularly self-definitions. Thus, the self becomes a Me exclusively, and conduct is held to be wholly predictable (in principle) on the basis of internalized prescriptions and proscriptions. If we know the actor's reference groups, according to Kuhn, we can predict his/her self-attitudes; and, if we know these, we can predict his/her behavior. In short, antecedent conditions determine the human being's self; and his/her self determines his/her conduct. This view, of course, conveniently disposes of such 'non-empirical' concepts as the I and impulses. At the same time, it preserves a premise that many consider indispensable to the scientific enterprise, that of determinism. In so doing, however, it sacrifices the processual character of the self and the negotiated character of behavior, points to which we shall soon devote attention.

If the preceding few paragraphs were exhaustive of the determinacy-indeterminacy controversy as it is manifested in the two schools, the matter might find a relatively easy resolution. Both standpoints might compromise simply by accepting a *probabilistic* frame of reference for human behavior. As the next several paragraphs will demonstrate, however, the controversy holds important implications for other substantive elements in the viewpoints of the two schools.

We have made passing reference, in the course of the preceding discussion, to related fundamental divergences in imagery. We now turn our attention to a more direct and fuller presentation of these divergences, placing them in the clarifying context of a process–structure distinction. The Chicago school tends to conceive of both self and society in processual terms, while the Iowa school stresses structural conceptions of both phenomena. These opposing views are clearly discernible in two very intimately related topics: (1) images of behavior as 'constructed' or as 'released,' and (2) images of role performance as 'role-making' or as 'role-playing.'

Blumer states his predilection for a processual image of human conduct and his repudiation of the structuralist image in the following terms (1953:199):

> the likening of human group life to the operation of a mechanical structure, or to the functioning of a system seeking equilibrium, seems to me to face grave difficulties in view of the formative and explorative character of interaction as the participants judge each other and guide their own acts by that judgment.

Similarly, as we have noted previously, he refers to the self as a flowing process of interaction between the I and the Me, and not merely a summation of the two aspects nor an organization of attitudes. This reflexive process is one in which the actor makes indications to himself/herself, that is to say, takes note of things and ascertains their import for his/her line of action. Action is seen to be built up, or constructed, in the course of its execution, rather than 'merely being released from a pre-existing psychological structure by factors playing on the structure' (Blumer, 1966:536). The conditions accounting for the action are not present at its beginning; for, 'with the mechanism of self-interaction the human being ceases to be a responding organism whose behavior is a product of what plays upon him from the outside, the inside, or both' (1966:535). Rather, he/she rehearses his/her behavior, summoning up plans of action, assessing them, changing them, and forming new ones, while indicating to himself/herself what his/her action will be. This tentative, exploratory process gives rise, we have suggested, to the possibility of novelty in behavior.

Although Kuhn has maintained that 'the individual is not merely a passive agent automatically responding to the group-assigned meanings of objects' (Hickman and Kuhn, 1956:26), he and his adherents are compelled by their methodological and deterministic commitments to deviate a bit from this disavowal. Conceiving the self as a structure of attitudes derived from the individual's internalized statuses and roles, they assign causal significance in behavior to these somewhat fixed attributes. That these elements are considered stable 'traits,' at least during a given time-period, is reflected in the use of the TST as a predictor of behavior without specification of the situations in which the test is administered or to which the predictions will be applied.[2] This same assumption of relative stability, or fixity, is found in Kuhn's implied notion of a 'core' self, as expressed in his assertion that: 'Central to an individual's conception of himself is his identity, that is, his generalized position in society . . .' (no date: 6). Omitting the I, impulses, or the spontaneous component of the self from his consideration, Kuhn is constrained to overlook the important process of interplay between the different aspects of the self.

The foregoing discussion implies divergent conceptions of the nature of role-behavior. These conceptions can be summarized as 'role-making,' which designates a tentative, dynamic, and creative process, and 'role-playing' (occasionally termed 'role-taking' by some writers), which designates behavior in response to the role expectations of others. Both D. Wrong (1961) and R. Turner (1962) have remarked upon the changing character of role theory. Originally, such theory depicted an exploratory and emergent interaction process, one marked by fluidity and, often, some degree of innovation. Increasingly, however, this theory has come to be linked with the concepts of 'status' and 'role-playing' and employed as a refinement of theories of conformity, or social control. Blumer resists this movement toward a collective determinism, describing human group life as a process of formative transactions. He sees cultural norms, status positions, and role relationships as only the frameworks within which social action takes place and not the crucial and coercive determinants of that action. With other members of the Chicago school, he conceives of the human being as creating or remaking his/her environment, as 'carving out' his/her world of objects, in the course of action—rather than simply responding to normative expectations.

As we have seen, Kuhn, in sharp contrast, conceives of personality as an organization of attitudes, which are, in effect, internalizations of the individual's role recipes. He describes the individual's roles as the norm in terms of which he/she structures objects and situations. Putting the matter quite succinctly, Kuhn writes (Hickman and Kuhn, 1956:45):

> As self theory views the individual, he derives his plans of action from the roles he plays and the statuses he occupies in the groups with which he feels identified—his reference groups. His attitudes toward himself as an object are the best indexes to these plans of action, and hence to the action itself, in that they are the anchoring points from which self-evaluations and other evaluations are made.

Anyone familiar with the TST, in which the assumption of conformity is implicit, will find no surprise in the foregoing statement. This assumption is foreshadowed, also, in an early (pre-TST) essay by Kuhn, in which he claims: 'Social and cultural factors become determinants of personality factors only as the individual comes to internalize the roles he plays and the statuses he occupies. He asks "Who am I?" and can answer this question of identity only in terms of his social position . . .' (1954:60). Even idiosyncratic elements in role-performance are fully explainable, for Kuhn, in terms of composites or resultants of the role-expectations held by the actor's various reference groups.

We see, then, that Blumer and Kuhn attribute different properties to the self, the former emphasizing the deliberate element, out of which a 'new' image may emerge, and the latter emphasizing more or less preset attitudes and responses. According to Blumer, the self is a process of internal conversation, in the course of which the actor can come to view himself/herself in a new way, thereby bringing about changes in himself/herself. Moreover, in his/her transactions with others, there occurs a continuing sequence of interpretation of the conduct of others, during which the actor may subject his/her attributes to highly variable use—or disuse. As Blumer puts it: 'The vital dependency of the attitude on the nature of the on-going interaction suggests how fallacious it is to use the attitude to construct the scheme of that interaction' (1953:193). Kuhn, on the other hand, characterizes both the self and human interaction as structured. The organized set of self-attitudes serves as a system of pre-established plans of action. And human association takes the form of fairly stable, ready-made patterns of role and counter-role prescriptions. For him, then, prescriptions of behavior and descriptions of behavior tend to coincide. Thus is social order maintained. The implications of these opposing conceptions, the processual and structural models of human social life, extend to such topics as the nature of socialization, social order, social control, social change, social disorganization, and social action generally.

Of the many other, relatively minor, points of differentiation between the schools, we shall select only one for consideration—that of the basic forms of human interaction. Although the disagreement is a clear-cut one, its implications are not very far-reaching. Hence, our discussion will be brief.

Following Mead, Blumer distinguishes two forms, or levels, of human interaction: symbolic interaction (which is uniquely and distinctively human) and non-symbolic interaction (which is shared with infrahuman organisms). The latter is a conversation of gestures, essentially of a stimulus-response nature, in which each organism responds to the perceived actions, or gestures, of the other without making efforts to ascertain the standpoint of the other. An example is provided by the vague feelings of uneasiness two persons may experience in one another's presence, feelings that may spiral in intensity even in the absence of symbolic behavior. Such interaction may arise from sources of which the actors are unaware and may involve either unwitting and unintended responses or responses to unindicated attributes of the other.

It is true that this level of interaction has received little theoretical attention and even less research attention from members of the Chicago school. But, it appears to have been completely ignored by the Iowa school. By focusing its concern upon the conduct of socialized persons, and viewing such conduct as responsive only to shared meanings, the latter school leaves no room for non-symbolic behavior. In view of this school's negation of the I concept, this omission is, of course, to be expected. What emerges, then, is a conception of human behavior and interaction as highly cognitive, non-affective phenomena. For all practical purposes, however, the divergence on this matter between the two schools is one of small degree rather than of kind.

Summarizing the issues dividing the Chicago and Iowa schools, we find them, upon close examination, to have an organic, systematic character. In making this point, it is useful to recall an argument we presented earlier: while Blumer's image of humans dictates his methodology, Kuhn's methodology dictates his image of humans. Thus, Blumer commences with a depiction of human behavior and interaction as emergent, processual, and voluntaristic, entailing a dialogue between impulses and social definitions, in the course of which acts are constructed. He pauses, however, to recognize a level of human interaction devoid of social definitions and reflecting sheerly spontaneous behavior. Holding these two preceding ideas, he exhibits skepticism regarding the extent to which human behavior is predictable. And, finally, in the light of the foregoing components of his imagery, he must insist upon a methodology that 'respects the nature of the empirical world,' relying upon a phenomenological approach, participant observation, and sensitizing concepts—all linked with a research 'logic of discovery.'

Oppositely, Kuhn begins with a scientific concern, stressing operationalism, the TST (a paper-and-pencil instrument), and definitive concepts—all linked with a 'logic of verification.' Although conjoined with his symbolic-interactionist orientation, this concern brings him to an acceptance of a basically deterministic image of human behavior. Bound to the service of scientism and determinism, he must deny to the I any role whatsoever in conduct, thereby dismissing the possibilities of both emergence and true voluntarism, on the one hand, and non-symbolic human interaction, on the other. In recognition of the magnitude of these modifications of symbolic interactionism, Kuhn relinquishes the customary name of that orientation in favor of 'self theory.'

It appears quite likely that these two schools of thought may continue their present tendency of taking little cognizance of one another and going their separate ways. This tendency is evidenced by the rarity with which representatives of each school cite the work of the other school. Fostering such parochialism and militating against the reconvergence of the Chicago and Iowa schools, is their fundamental and irreconcilable divergence on the methodological level.

THE DRAMATURGICAL APPROACH[3]

The major exponent of the dramaturgical approach in symbolic interactionism has been E. Goffman. While obtaining two graduate degrees from the University of Chicago, he gained exposure to Blumer, E. C. Hughes, and W. L. Warner (as well as other mentors) and, through them, to the influential ideas of Mead, Durkheim, and Simmel. It is from these latter that he appears to have derived the inspiration for his views on the reality-constructing behavior of humans, the pervasive significance of ceremony and ritual in human social life, and the utility of a 'formal' orientation that overlooks historical specificities in a quest for universal generalizations. His approach shows greater affinity, both substantively and methodologically, for the Chicago than for the Iowa school. Commenting upon a related matter, Lofland (1970:38) refers to Goffman's prolific invention of 'mini-concepts' and credits (or blames) the 'conceptually impoverished symbolic interactionist tradition at the University of Chicago in the later forties and early fifties.'

The point of departure for Goffman's dramaturgical metaphor, derived partly from the influential ideas of the philosopher-critic K. Burke (especially 1945 and 1950), is the premise that when human beings interact each desires to 'manage' the impressions the others receive of him/her. In effect, each puts on a 'show' for the others. The preface of Goffman's first monograph in the 'life as theater' vein puts the matter as follows (1959:xi):

> The perspective employed in this report is that of the theatrical performance; the principles derived are dramaturgical ones. I shall consider the way in which the individual . . . presents himself and his activity to others, the ways in which he guides and controls the impressions they form of him, and the kinds of things he may and may not do while sustaining his performance before them.

Thus, interactants, singly or in 'teams,' give 'performances,' during which they enact 'parts,' or 'routines,' which make use of a 'setting' and 'props,' as well as both the 'front region' of the 'scene' and the 'back-stage' (hidden from the 'audience'). The outcome of each performance is an imputation by the audience of a particular kind of self to the performed character(s). This imputation is as much, or more, a product of the expressive, ritualistic, or ceremonial elements in the actor's behavior as of the instrumental, practical, or substantive elements.

The core aspect of the actor's histrionics is presented in another statement by Goffman (1959:15):

> I assume that when an individual appears before others he will have many motives for trying to control the impressions they

receive of the situation. This report is concerned with some of the common techniques that persons employ to sustain such impressions and with some of the common contingencies associated with the employment of these techniques . . . I shall be concerned only with the participant's dramaturgical problems of presenting the activity before others.

As Goffman points out, 'Information about the individual helps to define the situation, enabling others to know in advance what he will expect of them and what they may expect of him' (1959:1). It is to the individual's advantage, of course, to present himself/herself in ways that will best serve his/her ends. In Goffman's analysis, then, the self becomes an object about which the actor wishes to foster an impression.

If we even cursorily scan the essays in one of Goffman's numerous books, we can give some further impressions of his orientation. *Interaction Ritual: Essays in Face-to-Face Behavior* (1967) furnishes a representative set of ideas. The first essay, 'On Face Work,' presents the keynote idea that human beings strive to interact with others in ways that maintain both their own 'face' and that of other interactants. Such management of impressions is the fundamental principle of the tacit norms governing such brief encounters as conversations, track meets, banquets, jury trials, street loitering, and the like. 'The Nature of Deference and Demeanor' draws upon Goffman's observations of mental patients to illustrate how deference represents the conveyance of regard or respect, and demeanor provides the means through which the actor creates an image of himself/herself for others. In 'Embarrassment and Social Organization,' Goffman describes situations in which some event threatens, challenges, or discredits the claims an actor has projected about himself/herself. The social function of embarrassment is shown to reside in the demonstration that the face-losing actor is at least disturbed by it and may prove more worthy another time. 'Alienation from Interaction' describes ways in which an actor may lose his/her involvement in a conversational encounter. Such 'misinvolvements' (e.g., external preoccupation, self-consciousness, etc.) violate the social requirement that interactants must elicit and sustain spontaneous involvement in a shared focus of attention. Challenging the view that psychotic behavior is a defect in information transmitting or in interpersonal relating, 'Mental Symptoms and Public Order' presents the view that symptomatic behavior may well been seen as a failure to conform to the tacit rules of decorum and demeanor that regulate interpersonal 'occasions.' 'Where the Action Is' employs the vocabulary of gambling in analyzing activities in which actors knowingly take avoidable risks. These activities provide special opportunities to establish and maintain face.

In common with the ethnomethodologists, whom we shall consider in a later section, Goffman recognizes that the norms regulating social conduct tend to escape notice, because they are taken for granted, and he stresses instances in which norms are violated in order to disclose what they are and how they are maintained. Collins and Makowsky describe this concern as 'the sociology of the common man,' often concentrating upon 'embarrassment, uneasiness, self-consciousness, awkward situations, *faux pas*, scandals, mental illness' (1972:202). Despite such concentration, however, Goffman's actors play their roles with minimal manifestations of love, hate, or other emotions.

Among the many commonalities of dramaturgy and the Chicago school, is their shared corrective to the conventional assumption that roles determine the behavior of interactants. Stressing the calculative and situational behavior of actors, both approaches remind us that norms, positions, and roles are simply the frameworks within which human interaction occurs. As we shall soon see, however, important differences obtain between these approaches as to how they portray role-performances. Goffman's concept of 'role distance'—the hiatus between the actor's role prescriptions and role performance—captures, in its overtones of cynicism, a significant component of this difference.

In his pursuit of the intricacies of impression-management in face-to-face situations, Goffman has relied upon sympathetic introspection as his method of observation and upon a felicitous style of presentation. Reactions to these aspects of his work have frequently employed such encomiums as 'insightful, sensitive observer,' 'stylistic elegance,' 'brilliant, provocative,' 'witty and graceful writing,' and so on. Other critical responses have been less favorable. His work has been criticized on theoretical, methodological, and ideological grounds. The emotive language comprising his style of presentation is quite compatible with his 'literary' methodology and its substantive products. We find in his work no explicit theory, but a plausible and loosely-organized frame of reference; little interest in explanatory schemes, but masterful descriptive analysis; virtually no accumulated evidence, but illuminating allusions, impressions, anecdotes, and illustrations; few formulations of empirically testable propositions, but innumerable provocative insights. In addition, we find an insufficiency of qualifications and reservations, so that the limits of generalization are not indicated. Duncan (1968) essays a heroic exercise in remedying the latter deficiency, presenting an inventory of 12 'axiomatic propositions,' 24 'theoretical propositions,' and 35 'methodological propositions.'

To many commentators, Goffman's scheme of imagery suggests a sordid, disenchanting view of humans and their society, one marked by both duplicity and despair. It is contended that this view celebrates the subordination of reality to appearance, of *Gemeinschaft* to pseudo-*Gemeinschaft*, of morality to opportunism. Thus, commentators refer to Goffman's views of the human being as 'an a-moral merchant of morality,' or as a 'detached, rational impression-manager,' and of the self 'as pure commodity.' Cuzzort, for example, scores the conceptions of 'humanity as the big con,' the 'reduction of humanity to an act or performance,' 'the "phony" element' in all social performances, and 'man as role player and manipulator of props, costumes, gestures, and words' (1969 : 175–92).

This conception of Goffman's imagery is cleverly described by Lyman and Scott, employing the titles of several of Goffman's published works (1970 : 20):

> Goffman's social actor, like Machiavelli's prince, lives externally. He engages in a daily round of impression management, presenting himself to advantage when he is able, rescuing what he can from a bad show. His everyday life consists of interaction rituals, employing deference and demeanor, saving his own and someone else's face, inhibiting actions that would spoil the fun in games, being intimate when occasion demands, maintaining his distance when proximity would be unwise, and in general being continuously alive to the requirements of behavior in public places.

Goffman's predecessors in the symbolic interactionist perspective (Mead, Dewey, Cooley, Thomas and others) gave no extensive consideration to impression management, insincerity, hypocrisy, or inauthentic self-presentations. His analysis advances, in effect, a significant reconstruction of the image of human beings offered in symbolic interactionism. In later paragraphs, we shall essay a possible explanation of this reconstruction. First, however, we shall touch upon a demurrer from the pejorative commentaries upon Goffman's metaphor and shall, also, describe a few more unfavorable criticisms of his views.

Messinger, et al. (1962), challenge the foregoing interpretation of Goffman's imagery, arguing that the dramaturgic analyst does not consider the theatrical model as representing his subjects' view of the world. The dramaturgical frame of reference is, rather, a device used by the analyst to focus attention upon the effects of the actor's behavior upon the perceptions of him/her by others. Whatever the actor's beliefs may be about what he/she is doing, the dramaturgist attends to the *impression* the actor has upon others. The analyst's frame of reference, then, may or may not comport with that used by the actor in viewing his/her own conduct. As a matter of fact, according to these defenders of Goffman, the very strength of dramaturgical analysis may reside in the discrepancy between the two frames of reference. For such discrepancy may enable the analyst to elucidate matters of which his/her subjects are unaware. Specifically, he/she may then reveal the way in which interactants construct, through their own acts, the 'reality' that they take for granted is 'out there.'

Some critics have attacked Goffman from another quarter, questioning his notion of the functional necessity of 'performances' in the maintenance of social order (Collins and Makowsky, 1972 : 212). In their view, the increasing informality of modern interpersonal relationships and the erosion of rank in contemporary American society raise doubts about the degree to which such rituals are essential to social life. In any event, there appears to be good reason for doubting the ubiquity of cool, calculating impression management in human affairs.

An intensive critique of Goffman's approach appears in a review, by Blumer, of one of the former's recent books. Blumer, while commending both the book and Goffman's work in general, discusses certain important weaknesses in the approach. These weaknesses (Blumer, 1972 : 52):

> stem from the narrowly constructed area of human group life that he has staked out for study. He has limited the area to face-to-face association with a corresponding exclusion of the vast mass of human activity falling outside of such association. Further, he has

confined his study of face-to-face association to the interplay of personal positioning at the cost of ignoring what the participants are doing.

In other words, the dramaturgical approach ignores the macrocosm within which its micro-level concerns are imbedded. Similarly, the approach overlooks the actual substantive content of human encounters in its concern exclusively with the expressive forms of the encounters. The resultant image of the human condition is a partial, truncated one. This defect is exacerbated by an assumption that human interaction is always organized and stable, an assumption that excludes dynamic, unstructured, and problematic interpersonal situations. Still, this assumption is occasionally bent (but not violated) by the analysis of such pathological incidents as social miscues and lapses.

How does Goffman come by his image of humans in society? One can make a good case for linking the genesis and popular appeal of the dramaturgical approach to the changing character of American society. We can point to mass society, with its mass production, mass marketing, and mass manipulation of tastes, as directing sociological attention to social appearances. As D. Martindale expresses it (1960 : 79):

> Since the days of James, Cooley, and Mead, the full implications of mass society have gradually become clear. . . . The old intimacy of small town image and incident disappears as the elaborate complexities of the mass societies are presupposed. The analysis shifts to social appearances and takes place in terms of roles, acts, scenes, and incidents. Man as an opportunist rather than moral agent is visualized operating at the center of his web. Both the religious and the humanistic view of man are excluded from the new theory.

A. Gouldner (1970a), in much the same vein, elaborates upon several interrelated societal sources of the dramaturgical metaphor. He points out that modern men and women are likely to be functionaries or clients of large-scale bureaucratic organizations over which they have little influence. This being the case, Goffman pays little attention to the efforts of people to alter the structure of such organizations. Further, in such organizations individuals tend to become readily interchangeable units whose sense of worth and power is, consequently, impaired. Lacking impact on the organizational structure and its functioning, they bend their efforts to the management of impressions that will maintain or enhance status. These efforts, Gouldner asserts plausibly, are more likely to be made by persons who retain individualistic and competitive orientations to life, but who are dependent for their livings upon large-scale organizations.

The newer, salaried middle classes are those most directly vulnerable to the conditions just described. Gouldner characterizes Goffman's dramaturgy as 'a revealing symptom of the latest phase in the long-term tension between the middle class's orientation to morality and its concern with utility' (1970a : 386). Constrained by the new exigencies, their faith in both utility and morality seriously undermined, the new middle class endeavors to 'fix its perspective in aesthetic standards, in the appearance of things' (390).

Gouldner suggests still another way in which the social situation described above impinges upon the dramaturgical view. Mirroring today's society, Goffman (as we have seen) focuses upon the episodic, or situational, upon micro-analysis of brief encounters, without reference to historical circumstances or institutional frameworks (390). This feature of Goffman's imagery is, of course, common to the varieties of contemporary symbolic interactionism.

The foregoing ideas about the social framework of dramaturgical analysis are not universally held. Brittan (1973 : 121–6) considers these ideas to be in error, for dramatic performances are, for him, a feature of all interaction, whether in preliterate or contemporary society. Humans, he contends, offer their audiences what they believe the audiences expect, trying to maximize the efficacy and power of their performances in order to maximize the social cohesion. The Durkheimian roots of this defense are readily evident.

We have seen that dramaturgical analysis has its detractors, chiefly on the basis of its ideologically unpalatable imagery and, to a lesser extent, its 'soft' methodology. This variety of interactionism, however, also has its equally ardent admirers. Among these, R. Collins and M. Makowsky are specially laudatory, perhaps extravagantly so. They applaud the dramaturgical perspective for making social behavior 'the central focus of attention, not in unrealistic laboratory situations, but in real-life encounters that make up the substance of society,' and they claim that for the first time there opens up a real possibility of sociology's becoming a science—a precise and rigorous body of knowledge . . .' (1972:213). To those who agree with this appraisal, Goffman's dramaturgical stance only partially accounts for it. Equally important are his contributions to the labeling perspective ('the dramatization of evil') on deviance, in *Stigma: Notes on the Management of Spoiled Identity* (1963), and his scintillating depiction of 'total institutions,' in *Asylums: Essays on the Social Situation of Mental Patients and Other Inmates* (1961).

ETHNOMETHODOLOGY

Several writers have discussed the affinities (for example: Denzin, 1969, 1970; Dreitzel, 1970; Petras and Meltzer, 1973; Wallace, 1969; Warshay, 1971) and the differences (for example: Deutscher, 1973; Douglas, 1970c; Heap and Roth, 1973; Hinkle, 1972; Zimmerman and Wieder, 1970) between ethnomethodology and symbolic interactionism. We agree with Wallace, who writes: 'Insofar as ethnomethodology embraces a theoretic (rather than methodologic) viewpoint, it is clearly symbolic interactionist' (1969:35). Hence, we shall examine ethnomethodology as a variation of the general interactionist perspective.

H. Garfinkel, leading progenitor of ethnomethodology, has been on the faculty of the University of California (Los Angeles) since 1954. From this post he has developed and led a group of thinkers (several now at the Santa Barbara branch of the University of California) who have felt themselves to be adherents of an embattled, 'encapsulated' speciality, targets of contemptuous rejection by mainstream American sociology. His intellectual precursors have included, most notably, A. Schutz, E. Husserl, M. Merleau-Ponty, A. Gurwitsch, and other phenomenologists, as well as various linguistic philosophers. Of these former, Schutz has been most influential in Garfinkel's thinking; but, T. Parsons, one of Garfinkel's mentors at Harvard during his doctoral studies, has also exerted important influence.[4]

Any attempt to grasp the nature of ethnomethodology must come to grips with Garfinkel's convoluted, opaque prose. Additionally, one must acquire a degree of facility with a large array of esoteric concepts, such as the following: 'bracketing,' 'deep rules,' 'documentation,' 'epoche,' 'et cetera clause,' 'glossing,' 'idealization,' 'reduction,' 'reflexivity,' 'second order conceptions,' 'typification,' etc. With this caution in mind, we shall follow the lead of P. Filmer (1972: 206–7) and present some of the many 'definitions,' or delimitations of ethno-methodology's scope offered by Garfinkel:

> Ethnomethodological studies analyze everyday activities as members' methods for making those same activities visibly-rational-and-reportable-for-all-practical-purposes, i.e. 'accountable,' as organizations of commonplace everyday activities. The reflexivity of that phenomenon is a singular feature of practical actions, of practical circumstances, of common sense knowledge of social structures, and of practical sociological reasoning. By permitting us to locate and examine their occurrence the reflexity of that phenomenon establishes their study.
>
> Their study is directed to the tasks of learning how members' actual, ordinary activities consist of methods to make practical actions, practical circumstances, common sense knowledge of social structures, and practical sociological reasoning analyzable; and of discovering the formal properties of commonplace, practical common sense actions, 'from within' actual settings, as ongoing accomplishments of those settings. The formal properties obtain their guarantees from no other source, and in no other way (1967: vii-viii).
>
> The following studies seek to treat practical activities, practical circumstances, and practical sociological reasoning as topics of empirical study, and by paying to the most commonplace activities of daily life the attention usually accorded extraordinary events, seek to learn about them as phenomena in their own right. Their central recommendation is that the activities whereby members produce and manage settings of organized everyday affairs are identical with members' procedures for making these settings 'account-able.' The 'reflexive,' or incarnate character of accounting practices and accounts make up the crux of that recommendation (1967: 1).
>
> I use the term 'ethnomethodology' to refer to the investigation of the rational properties of indexical expressions and other practical actions as contingent ongoing accomplishments or organized artful practices of everyday life (1967: 11).

Given the ponderous and difficult character of Garfinkel's writing, we shall limit further quotations from his works. Much of the following material will expatiate upon the implications of the foregoing definitions. As the first step towards such expatiation, we shall briefly summarize the book from which the definitions are quoted, Garfinkel's sole published book to date (1967).

An introductory chapter 'What Is Ethnomethodology?' illustrates the approach by examining the contingencies and practices that shape decisions in coding cases of suspected suicide. We learn that, despite definite and elaborate rules, in each case 'et cetera,' 'unless,' 'let it pass,' and 'factum valet' understandings come into play in the actual coding. The seven following essays (three of them published previously) provide further illustrations. 'Studies of the Routine Grounds of Everyday Activities' describes observations and experiments, by students in Garfinkel's classes, whereby the background understandings that are taken for granted in commonplace conversations and incidents are disclosed. The chief technique of experimentation is that of disrupting the smooth flow of routine events. In 'Common Sense Knowledge of Social Structures: the Documentary Method of Interpretation in Lay and Professional Fact Finding,' we see how persons who are led to believe that they are receiving counseling on personal problems manage to make sense of random 'yes' and 'no' responses to their questions by pseudo-counselors. 'Some Rules of Correct Decisions that Jurors Respect' reports on the methods used by jury members to negotiate resolutions of differences between legal rules and everyday rules. One of Garfinkel's more notorious studies is reported in 'Passing and the Managed Achievement of Sex Status in an Intersexed Person.' Based upon interviews with a male transvestite, the paper describes the techniques by which the subject adapted to the development of female secondary sex characteristics. In an appendix to the paper, Garfinkel confesses to having been duped by the subject into believing that these characteristics developed spontaneously, whereas later information revealed that the subject had been taking estrogens surreptitiously. 'Good Organizational Reasons for "Bad" Clinic Records' clarifies how case records (of the outpatient Psychiatric Clinic at the U.C.L.A. Medical Center) may be quite useful only for staff-members (who have the necessary background understandings) while being virtually useless for actuarial or research purposes. What appears to be Garfinkel's most ambitious essay, replete with interesting diagrams and statistical tables, is 'Methodological Adequacy in the Quantitative Study of Selection Criteria and Selection Activities in Psychiatric Outpatient Clinics.' Here we find an analysis of the actual decision-making process in selecting outpatients for treatment and for discharge. The final paper, 'The Rational Properties of Scientific and Common Sense Activities,' challenges the applicability of the conventional scientific method to an understanding of the banalities of everyday life.

What each of these essays accomplishes on a small scale, Cicourel's *The Social Organization of Juvenile Justice* (1968) does more fully in an intensive, thorough study. Cicourel succeeds in revealing, more fully than previous investigators using different theoretical frameworks and methods, the artifactual character of juvenile delinquency. Examining the everyday routines of discretionary behavior by police, probation officers, court officials, and school personnel, he minutely documents the 'creation' of delinquency. Additional ethnomethodological investigations are those by Sudnow (1967), McHugh (1968), and MacAndrew and Edgerton (1969).

In his comments on this variant of symbolic interactionism, L. Churchill (1971 : 183) notes that 'the ethnomethodologist continually asks the technical question "How is that social activity done?"' Ethnomethodology, thus, concerns itself with the process by which we understand the world; hence, it examines human behavior on both the conscious and, more importantly, taken-for-granted levels. An excellent summary of the position by P. Filmer (1972 : 203–34) stresses the following ideas. Commonplace (everyday, taken-for-granted) activities are characterized by an implicit order that emerges in the course of interaction and the activity itself. This order functions to make situations 'accountable,' that is, explainable or understandable. Much of our daily activity, for example, assumes the existence of an 'et cetera clause,' whereby our expressions (verbal and non-verbal) imply a continued directive towards a given type of social activity that is not explicitly stated. Filmer (1972 : 210) makes it clear that :

> according to ethnomethodology, sociology is the study of all aspects of everyday social life, however trivial they may seem, just as much as it is the study of extraordinary events; and . . . sociology is, in an important sense, itself an everyday activity.

We have noted the debt owed to the earlier work of the phenomenologists, especially A. Schutz. However, ethnomethodology attempts to move beyond the understanding of human behavior in terms of the meanings constructed by each individual in social interaction, to a systematic search ('documentary interpretation') for the ways in which shared meanings ('indexical expressions') come to be taken for granted in human society (see Psathas, 1968). The basic position of this approach entails, of course, a processual view of human society. Everyday reality continually undergoes construction; for, although humans act in terms of a naïve realism, they must actively negotiate each social situation in terms of problematic subjective interpretations.

We should like to point out two significant departures of ethnomethodology from the general interactionist tradition. Dreitzel indicates one of these, noting that ethnomethodologists, unlike most other interactionists, maintain that: 'the social order, including all its symbols and meanings, exists not only precariously but has no existence at all independent of the members' accounting and describing practices' (1970:xv). The implied thorough-going idealism and solipsism are suggested in Cooley's views but vigorously denied in Mead's. In any case, the focus of ethnomethodology 'is not on activity but rather on the process by which members manage to produce and sustain a sense of social structure' (Mullins, 1973:195).

Secondly, ethnomethodology has established itself as an important force in the rise, or resurgence, over the past few years, of the sociology of sociology. In works by Cicourel (1964) and Douglas (1970a; 1970b) we find depictions of the flimsy nature of social reality in general society, as well as indications of the ways in which sociologists construct with each other an equally flimsy social reality. This latter enterprise often gives rise to the assumption by sociologists of certain givens that hinder efforts to understand social conduct from the perspective of the actor.

Thus, to assume the existence of a social reality actually 'out there' appears to be universal. As 'social realities' emerge relative to our particular position in social and cultural matrixes, exactly what system of reality is defined as warranting our trust varies. This assumed reality, in turn, defines the ways in which the relationships themselves are interpreted and carried out during interaction. Ethnomethodologists are interested in the 'methods' used by the observed and the observer alike for dealing with their everyday life realities (see, for example, Collins and Makowsky, 1972:209).

So, ethnomethodology closely approximates to the Chicago school in methodological preferences, with emphasis upon sympathetic introspection and participant-observer research. The ethnomethodologists, however, have shown, in many instances, a greater cognizance of the role of history in behavior, as well as such traditional interactionist concerns as time, place, and situation (see, for example, Warshay, 1971 : 25). Needless to say, such cognizance has its defects as well as its virtues, rendering trans-situational generalization problematic. Generally speaking, however, interactionism has been notably ahistorical, with little follow-up of the types of analyses appearing in Mead's *Movements of Thought in the Nineteenth Century* (1936). We shall conclude our consideration of ethnomethodology by briefly examining the image of humans portrayed in the writings of that variety of interactionism.

Much of the criticism leveled against ethnomethodology is directed at it as both a sociological theory and a methodological approach. For example, ethnomethodology has been castigated for ignoring relationships between individuals and larger social units, for offering no clear demonstration of how taken-for-granted assumptions operate in interaction, and for a lack of precision in explicating the documentary method (Denzin, 1969 : 929). One attempt to rebut the first of these criticisms, a criticism launched against the interactionist framework generally, is described by Dreitzel (1970). He contends that ethnomethodology 'tends to cut off all macrosociological considerations *for the time being* in order to concentrate on the basic rules of everyday communication and interaction' (x, our emphasis). Ethnomethodologists claim, he writes : 'Until we have understood how we . . . understand each other, all further sociological inquiry will be useless' (1970 : x).

Gouldner, however, touches upon what seems to us to be an even more serious criticism, one that involves ideological considerations, rather than the traditional problems of theory and research. In *The Coming Crisis in Western Sociology* (1970a : 395), Gouldner puts forward the view that, 'Garfinkel's is a sociology more congenial to the activistic 1960s and particularly to the more politically rebellious campuses of the present period.' Warshay, too, opines (1971 : 25) that ethnomethodology is a sociology of involvement at all levels. More than that, however, it is often a sociology of instigation. Whereas Goffman appears content merely to study the drama of coping with the depersonalization and alienation prevalent in modern society, Garfinkel and his cohorts often deliberately inflict these conditions upon others. Demonstrations of the acquisition of power by disrupting taken-for-granted assumptions, e.g., not accepting statements at their face value, bargaining for fixed-value items in a store, and falsely purporting to help individuals with personal problems (Garfinkel,

1967:62–71 and Chapter Three), all position the investigator as a superordinate manipulator and his subjects as mystified dupes. Thus, Goffman's opportunist becomes Garfinkel's blundering fool, trusting in something that isn't there, willfully destroyed by those pretending to share his/her trust.

SUMMARY

We have presented a brief overview of four of the most prominent varieties of contemporary symbolic interactionism. These approaches have been shown to differ not only in terms of what they consider to be the appropriate theoretical stance of interactionism but also in terms of the image of humans that results from, and interacts with, that particular stance.

In the Chicago school's orientation we find a conception of human beings as active agents in creating the social environment which, in turn, influences their behavior. The school's preferred methodology for understanding human behavior remains an unattained ideal in sociology. At present, research techniques are not adequately attuned to in-depth analysis of this unique feature of human conduct. The Iowa school, on the other hand, by insisting upon faithful adherence to positivism, has imaged relatively passive 'human beings as internalizers,' studying verbally expressed products of internalization. The dramaturgical approach has added a new dimension to the interactionist tradition—the manipulative penchant of humans. This focus has drawn attention to the taken-for-granted world in which the rituals of impression management are enacted. In doing so, the approach has laid a foundation for study of the 'world of everyday life' that provides the subject matter of ethnomethodology.

We must note, albeit belatedly, that our application of the label 'schools' to these varieties is not intended to imply that theorists and researchers working within each perspective necessarily define themselves as adherents to the given perspective. Parenthetically, it should be clear that the Chicago and Iowa schools refer to intellectual perspectives, not to geographical locations. Two 'deviant cases' that illustrate this point are A. Rose, who studied with Blumer at Chicago, and N. Denzin, who received his doctorate from the State University of Iowa. In general, it seems to us that members of the Iowa school share little in the nature of a consciousness of kind. We conjecture that this is due primarily to the circumstance that the major thrust of this approach incorporates, rather than differentiates it from, the mainstream of American sociological theory and research. Members of the Chicago school, in contrast, appear to be much more conscious of their distinctive theoretical and methodological position. Similarly, Goffman and his disciples stand forth as clearly identifiable. Among the ethnomethodologists, defined by themselves and by others as most at variance with current American sociology, self-identification is most highly salient; for, as Deutscher expresses it, 'They see themselves as a new discipline—a radical perspective on human behavior and its study' (1973 : 357).

Having surveyed these different orientations within modern interactionism, we are in a position to indicate one common element that has been connoted by much of our discussion but now merits explicit mention. We have in mind the important point that human interaction is a process of sharing one another's behavior rather than of merely responding to each other's words and actions. Such sharing is indispensable to, part and parcel of, the formation of a common world by members of any human group.

chapter 3

Criticisms of symbolic interactionism

This brief exposition of symbolic interactionism concludes on a critical note. Fairly numerous and rather diverse criticisms of both specific symbolic interactionists and symbolic interactionism in general are to be found in the sociological literature. Such criticisms range from a general dissection of the basic philosophical assumptions that underlie symbolic interactionism, whose origins are to be found in American pragmatism, to a detailed mapping of numerous sociological inadequacies and points of theoretical confusion found in the works of a single representative of the interactionist tradition.

We wish to begin this concluding section by, first, establishing a list of some representative criticisms, most of them recent, both of symbolic interactionism and of certain symbolic interactionists. Here our coverage will deal almost exclusively with present-day inter-actionists. Following the listing, we shall examine these critical commentaries in an attempt to assess whether they tend to be of specific 'types' such that many of them can meaningfully be grouped together. Those which can be so grouped will be discussed in some detail. The only classification we intend to impose on our initial listing of critical views is that distinguishing between those which originate with thinkers within the paradigm and those whose origins lie outside the framework. As we have presented numerous positive comments and criticisms in chapters 1 and 2, the criticisms to be dealt with here will be largely of a negative nature.

IN-HOUSE CRITICISMS

While there are a number of casual criticisms and occasional self-critical remarks to be found in the writings of symbolic interactionists, only two writers, B. N. Meltzer (1959; 1972) and A. Brittan (1973) have presented their critical statements in systematic fashion. While, as previously stated, it is our intention to deal with critiques of *contemporary* symbolic interactionists, we have elected to include Meltzer's critical statements because they are aimed directly at symbolic interactionism's most illustrious progenitor, its real founder, Mead. Brittan's criticisms, on the other hand, are not directed at any specific interactionist but are an 'insider's' analysis of symbolic interactionism in general. These two sets of criticisms, then, should provide us with a good starting point.

Meltzer's (1959; 1972 : 18–21) overall critique of Mead's social psychology can be summarized as follows :

1 Numerous major concepts in Mead's framework are either fuzzy and vague or are not employed with the consistency required in scientific explanation. Concepts particularly susceptible to such imprecise and varying definition include impulse, meaning, mind, role-taking, the I, self, self-consciousness, generalized other, object, image, attitude, gesture, and symbol. Such imprecisely defined concepts, requiring as they do an 'intuitive' understanding, are produced both by the fragmentary nature of many of Mead's ideas and by his emergent perspective on human behavior.

2 Mead's theory suffers from certain substantive omissions. Most of these omissions, in turn, derive from the fact that Mead's framework is one of form devoid of content. Among the more serious of these errors is a nearly total ignoring of the emotional and unconscious elements in human conduct.

3 Mead's theory gives rise to certain methodological difficulties. The framework is not one that is easily researched, and it contains no clearcut prescriptions of either general procedures or specific techniques for enhancing its researchability. Furthermore, Mead offers little in the way of empirical support for his position.

Brittan's (1973 : 190–204) criticisms of the general symbolic interaction perspective are summarized below :

1 Interactionism places an over-emphasis on self-consciousness; it 'plays down,' ignores, or makes light of both the unconscious and emotive factors as they influence the interactive process.

2 Symbolic interactionism is guilty of an unwarranted demotion of the psychological; it has robbed human needs, motives, intentions, and aspirations of their empirical and analytical reality by treating them as mere derivations and/or expressions of socially defined categories.

3 The interactionist perspective has come to have an obsession

with meaning. The social world is too often viewed as a mere adjunct to symbolic analysis, and both social change and social structure are lightly treated.

4 Interactionists too often see only the pejorative implications of the fragmentation of self, and they too readily assume that multiple identities are merely the unfortunate and dysfunctional end-products of a fragmented system of human relationships. The positive adaptive aspects of a multiple identity are seldom given the attention they would appear to warrant.

5 Symbolic interactionism's relativistic analysis of social inter-action often results in an over-emphasis on the situation and an obsessive concern with the transient, episodic, and fleeting.

6 Interactionism espouses a metaphysic of meaning. There is a danger that a fetish will be made out of everyday life, especially if the perspective comes to give a totally relativistic account of human interaction.

In admittedly truncated form, then, these are Meltzer's and Brittan's criticisms, and they are the major 'in-house,' or reflexive, critiques. Again, let us point out that Meltzer's critique of Mead is not necessarily meant to apply to symbolic interactionism *per se*, while Brittan's remarks, which are both more recent and more influ-enced by non-interactionists' critiques, are so intended. Furthermore, Brittan's fourth criticism, which he terms the pejorative implication of the fragmentation thesis, appears to apply only to the Chicago school of interactionism, for they are the specific interactionists who argue most forcefully for a unitary rather than a multiple conception of self. This specific criticism hardly seems applicable to such inter-actionists as A. and C. Rose (1969:65) or E. Goffman (1959), who are pleased to see the self as a multiple entity in all societies at all times. The one key point made by both Meltzer and Brittan deals with the failure, of both Mead and the general interactionist framework he outlined, to come to grips with either human emotions or the unconscious.

Meltzer and Brittan are not, of course, the only interactionists who have critically viewed their own perspective. For example, in detail-ing his list of criticisms, Meltzer (1972:19–20) acknowledges that he has drawn upon W. Kolb's trenchant critique of Mead's ambiguous usage of the concepts 'I' and 'Me,' as well as H. Blumer's contention that Mead did little to develop the methodological implications of his position and that his framework is an analytical one lacking in

substantive content. In addition, there are other symbolic interactionists whose critical comments, while not as systematically
stated, deserve to be included in our listing of 'in-house' criticisms.
We must add to our inventory the commentaries of N. K. Denzin
(1969), M. H. Kuhn (1964), and P. Hall (1972).

We begin with the critical commentary of Kuhn, whose remarks
are earlier, better known, and more systematically presented than
those of either Denzin or Hall. Kuhn's (1964:61–84) comments can
be summarized as follows:

1 Symbolic interactionism has suffered far too long from being
what, in fact, can only be labeled an 'oral tradition.' For years, most
of interactionism's key, or cardinal, ideas have been simply handed
down and spread around by word of mouth. During this long phase
of its development, interactionists were primarily concerned with
getting things 'down pat,' to learn the litany, to erect the system, and
to debate over its correct interpretation. This is an essentially unpro-
ductive period, in that 'whatever intellectual powers there may be,
are more devoted to casuistry and criticism than to inquiry and
creativity' (1964:62). While much of this 'oral tradition' emphasis
began to pass away with the posthumous publication of the major
works of G. H. Mead, 'the oral tradition has some tendency to continue in symbolic interactionism' (1964:63).

2 Following the general decline of the oral tradition, symbolic
interactionism entered an era of productive inquiry—an era characterized by a great increase in research and scholarly activity. However, this productive period, beginning in the early 1940s, has been
something of a mixed blessing. For, while it has indeed been an era
of inquiry, 'the inquiry has been directed at the testing and developing of what amounts almost to a welter of subtheories going by a
variety of names other than symbolic interactionism' (1964:63).
This plethora of theories and subtheories (i.e. self theory, role theory,
reference group theory, social perception and person perception
theories, the interpersonal theory of H. S. Sullivan, and the Whorf-
Sapir-Cassirer language and culture orientation), while perhaps indirectly contributing to interactionism, served both to confuse and
confound the development of a basic symbolic interactionist stance.
There are, then, a host of partial perspectives, or orientations, which,
because they bear varying relationships to the symbolic interactionist
framework, contribute little to clarifying or making more manageable
the general orientation. This 'welter of subtheories' is due, in large

part, to the way in which the issues of determinacy and indeterminacy are handled in Mead's original, overall orientation—which brings us to the third of Kuhn's criticisms.

3 There is a good deal of ambiguity in Mead's writings over the extent to which human behavior is determined, as opposed to its being 'determining.' The key source of such ambiguity is to be located in Mead's discussion of the self and its constituent elements the I and the Me. According to Kuhn (1964 : 64–5), one finds in Mead's work, depending on when and where one looks at it, the following divergent conceptions of the nature of the I and the Me :

> The notion that the I is indeterminate but the *me's* are determinate; the notion that both the I and *me's* are indeterminate; the notion that whereas both the I and *me's* are determinate results of identifiable events, the interaction (conversation) between the two is somehow itself indeterminate or emergent.

Such ambiguity continues to influence contemporary interactionism negatively by producing a situation in which no basic agreement can be reached with respect to how the perspective's most fundamental concepts should be defined. And this brings us to the fourth of Kuhn's basic criticisms.

4 The ambiguity concerning the determinacy-indeterminacy issue found in Mead's varying conceptions and discussions of self manifests itself in contemporary symbolic interactionism by way of producing nine possible alternative working definitions of the self. These varying, conflicting, and, in some cases, competing definitions of the concept self have, according to Kuhn, produced nine basic types of symbolic interaction theory. One result of all this is that symbolic interactionists cannot achieve even a minimal degree of consensus on the nature and meaning of a concept very closely associated with their orientation, the concept of self.

Kuhn's remaining three criticisms appear not to be linked together or to logically imply one another to the extent that his first four do.

5 Symbolic interactionism tends to remain somewhat asociological to the degree that the traditional symbolic interactionist framework has employed an individual, rather than a sociological, model of the social act. It is an individual model of the social act, by Kuhn's reasoning, for it is 'triggered by organic tensions and impulses and following through the course of the action with reference to the single—almost feral—man to equilibrium, restitution of tensionless-

ness in the organism' (1964:73). In Kuhn's opinion, this may not be a telling criticism, for he seems to believe that this defect may already have been remedied by the dramaturgical school of K. Burke and E. Goffman. The dramaturgists have made symbolic interactionism more sociological by eschewing the individual model of the social act in favor of a 'team-of-players model which implies that social agenda rather than tissue conditions serve to initiate the act and to cue its end as well' (1964:73). This seems to us a strange criticism of 'traditional' interactionism in view of the fact that, for Mead at least, the social act often—and in a sense always—implied joint action. Mead's conception of the social act was always more thoroughly and profoundly sociological than, for example, Weber's notion that the only requirement for an act to be social was subjective intention. Furthermore, in Weber's scheme, the individual habitually orients himself/herself to the expectations of others and never, as he/she does for Mead, engages in an internal conversation, i.e. interacts with himself/herself. And yet Goffman's image of the human being as always trying to 'pull off' a good performance in the attempt to convince others of the authenticity of one's self seems in this respect to be closer to Weber than to Mead. The crux of the matter is that we fail to see how such a conception of the social act as Mead's, a conception which accounts for both joint action and intra-individual interaction, is any less sociological than Weber's, which views the social act as a form of status-seeking, or Goffman's, which is not markedly dissimilar to Weber's. We have already criticized the dramaturgical interactionists' conception of sociology in chapter 2, and we shall return to it later.

6 Symbolic interactionism is beset with a number of pressing problems which have too long been neglected. Perhaps none of these 'neglected problems' is as pressing as the lack of sound thought and substantive, empirical research into the 'process by which self-conceptions change' (1964:78). The seriousness of this problem may be lessening now, according to Kuhn, because : 'We have arrived at the point in sharpening of the tools by which we may identify self-attributes and measure them and compare them with those of others, where we may treat this issue as a researchable question' (1964:78). It is worth noting at this point that, for Kuhn, ideas that are, for other interactionists, foci of ideological debates and substantive disagreements become transmuted into mere methodological issues.

7 In addition to the problem of a paucity of research into the specific processes by which self-conceptions change, one of inter-

actionism's more important neglected problems lies in its 'failure to make appropriate conceptualization of the varieties of functional relations that regularly occur between self and other' (1964:78). Furthermore, Kuhn argues that interactionists must come to agree on the precise terms which are to be used for each of the different relationships found to exist between self and other. Such agreement is necessary if interactionism is to operationalize its pivotal concepts. Kuhn's (1954:221-2) neopositivistic concern with the desirability of conceptual consensus is clearly stated in his own attempt to construct a working definition of the concept self: 'But now that the major difficulty—lack of agreement about the class of phenomena to be investigated—has been solved by the growing consensus that "the self" is a set of attitudes, we are able to bring to bear on our investigation of the self the techniques for studying attitudes in general.'

It should be noted again here that, at bottom, most of Kuhn's comments are criticisms of a methodological nature; he is critical of theoretical and substantive portions of symbolic interactionism to the extent that they pose methodological problems. This is the common thread which ties together all his criticisms into a single package—a package which is basically a critique of the Chicago style of interactionist reasoning and research and, at the same time, an expression of a conception of what interactionism ought to be, a conception that has come to be called the Iowa school.

N. K. Denzin's (1969) negative comments on symbolic interactionism can be listed with relative ease. However, in the course of preparing the ground for a presentation of his own critical views, Denzin lists, and then dismisses, a set of strictures which other critics have voiced. While Denzin does not mention the authors of these complaints, we have already identified some of these authors as Meltzer, Blumer, and Kuhn, and we shall see others when we compile our listing of critiques by 'outsiders.' Denzin (1969:929) mentions both criticisms which have been directed at symbolic interactionism in general and at interactionism's dramaturgical genre in particular:

1 The concept 'self' is so vaguely and ambiguously defined that good empirical observations cannot be made.

2 The perspective offers only a small number of concrete hypotheses.

3 Interactionism does not provide an adequate treatment of large-scale forms of social organization.

4 The dramaturgical school of interactionism 'gives man an un-attractive motivational commitment—that is, to ever win support for a presented self' (1969:929).

In the course of comparing and contrasting symbolic interactionism and ethnomethodology, Denzin notes what he personally feels are the 'failures' of both frameworks:

1 They fail to indicate clearly the true source(s) of those definitions and meanings which are considered crucial to an understanding of human behavior.

2 They fail to provide firm strategies for the assessment and measurement of the interaction process.

The second of these two 'failures' closely parallels selected remarks made by both Kuhn and Meltzer. At least one of the criticisms that Denzin attributes to others will be treated in greater depth when we take up the critical commentary of non-interactionists. We turn now to a brief consideration of an animadversion against symbolic inter-actionists that has captured the attention of P. Hall.

Hall's (1972) commentary is directed not at symbolic interactionism *per se*, but at numerous symbolic interactionists—truly numerous, as Hall argues that until very recently no symbolic interactionist had really dealt with the political system. However, in Hall's opinion, there is nothing endemic in the perspective itself which would lead it to be as apolitical as it has been. In fact, Hall sets out to demonstrate through his own work and writing that symbolic interactionism is, indeed, more than capable of handling political phenomena in a satisfactory fashion. It is in this light that he informs us that (1972: 70):

> The potential contribution of this approach has been ignored because sociology incorporated what was congruent and ignored contradiction and because critics superficially wrote off the perspective as being unresearchable, micro-level, overly subjective, indeterministic, lacking content and unsystematized.

By Hall's reasoning, then, not only is symbolic interactionism not inherently apolitical, but (1972:70):

> The paradigm . . . is ideally suited to handling the inevitable sources, manifestations, processes, and consequences of conflict and change. It seems designed to deal with the vitality and reality of a social life which has a political system that never stops or runs

down but faces new contingencies, issues, groups, conditions, and decisions as well as the reinterpretation of formerly rationalized matters.

Hall then proceeds to provide his own symbolic–interactionist analysis of politics. And while Hall warns us that his analysis of political processes and structures is only 'rudimentary and can only be seen as sensitizing and orienting' (1972:75), his analysis nevertheless deserves some comment. In all fairness to Hall, and realizing that he is precisely correct in labeling his analysis rudimentary and sensitizing, we shall not address our remarks to what Hall in fact has dealt with but rather to what he has omitted. What Hall has essentially dealt with is social process, what he has ignored or treated lightly is social structure. Furthermore, Hall is well aware that this is exactly what he has done; he realizes full well that his critics feel he deals with only relatively trivial political matters like electoral politics and collective behavior, and he even informs us that, 'my Marxist friends have criticized me for ignoring imperialism, capitalism, and class. . . .' (1972:75). In response to his Marxist critics, Hall contends that 'the position taken here [is] that . . . the material . . . elements come to be reflected in and expressed through the interpretive processes of the self-conceptions of the actors' (1972:75). But, of course, Hall does not tell us *how* the material elements come to be expressed through the interpretive processes of the self-conceptions of the actors; for, in order to do so he would have to locate these actors in the most crucial positions they occupy in the social structure. To locate actors in their most crucial positions is to deal with both capitalism and social class, but Hall prefers not to do this. He speaks instead of self-interest, but he fails to see the congruence between self-interest and class interest. Again, Hall simply asserts that material elements are expressed though the interpretive processes of the self-conceptions of the actors; he does not demonstrate it.

Whether or not symbolic interactionism is inherently apolitical is still an open question. Hall is quite correct in asserting that interactionists have not provided a satisfactory analysis of political processes and structures. Neither his article 'A Symbolic Interactionist Analysis of Politics' nor A. M. Rose's book, *The Power Structure* (1967), provides us with a remedy to this deficiency.

This concludes our brief listing of 'self-critical' analyses of symbolic interactionism. We do not, of course, claim that our composite listing is exhaustive. For example, we have omitted such older criticisms of individual interactionists as Mead's assessment of C. H. Cooley's utopianism and such recent critiques as Blumer's comments on Goffman's cynicism. We have, however, attempted to provide a representative set of critical comments and analyses.

Of the critical comments we have listed, there are four which appear with some frequency in the critiques of the 'insiders.' Three of these criticisms are truly insider views, for they have originated with writers working within the paradigm. The fourth criticism—that interactionism either ignores or plays down the influence of social organization—does not originate from within the perspective. We shall defer treatment of this specific criticism in any great detail until we take up the critiques by 'outsiders.' We shall see that this matter constitutes a quite formidable attack upon the utility of the interactionist perspective.

The remaining three criticisms can be summarized as follows:

1 Symbolic interactionism is beset with numerous methodological problems, i.e. its concepts are difficult to operationalize; it generates too few really testable hypotheses; its concepts and cardinal ideas too often have to be intuitively grasped rather than being readily apparent or easily made so; and it has failed to clearly spell out its specific methodological procedures.

2 One of interactionism's key concepts, the concept of self, is the object of much confusion in the writings of both past and present symbolic interactionists. The self is defined in numerous, and often conflicting, ways by both past and contemporary representatives of the paradigm; and, in fact, the self is sometimes defined and employed in inconsistent fashion by the same interactionist within the confines of a single article, text, or manuscript.

3 Interactionism has neglected both the affective and unconscious components of human behavior in constructing its overall picture of humans.

It is difficult to formulate a meaningful response to these three basic criticisms in the space we have allotted ourselves here, but we shall nevertheless provide enough commentary to indicate the extent to which we agree with each. Let us reverse the order in which the criticisms are summarized and address our first set of remarks to the charge that symbolic interactionism has neglected to deal with human emotions and the unconscious.

We find ourselves in basic agreement with this criticism, but it does not quite tell the whole story. That part of the criticism which applies to interactionism's neglect of the emotional element in human behavior needs some modification. While such emotions as love, hate, anger, joy, and sorrow have received little attention from contemporary interactionists, certain other emotions have been studied. These latter include the sentiments, those emotions which Cooley characterized as intimately involving 'sympathy,' or taking the role of the other. For example, Goffman (1967 : 97–112), as well as E. Gross and G. Stone (1964), have written on embarrassment, K. Riezler (1943) has analyzed shame, and, of course, Cooley was profoundly concerned with the nature of 'self-feeling.' Perhaps the importance of the role-taking component in shame, embarrassment, and self-feeling explains why these affective phenomena have been singled out for scrutiny by symbolic interactionists. There seems to be no reason to assume, however, that interactionism is not equally capable of dealing with other emotions. While the index to Mead's *Mind, Self and Society* contains only two references to human emotions, it should be remembered that Cooley, James, and Dewey did indeed deal with a wide range of emotions. It seems safe to state, however, that the founding fathers of symbolic interactionism directed more attention to human emotions than do contemporary interactionists.

The observation that interactionism has failed to come to grips with the 'unconscious' is truly well-founded and requires no modification. Aside from an occasional reference to the concept of 'levels of consciousness,' in which one such level 'comes close' to touching upon the unconscious, it is most 'difficult to find a considered discussion of the idea of the "unconscious" in the writings of symbolic interactionists' (Meltzer, 1972 : 576). And, as Meltzer (1972 : 576) further indicates: 'The few references we do find tend to renounce the concept without substituting adequate explanatory principles.' One symbolic interactionist does give credence to the role of the unconscious in structuring behavior, and he goes so far as to state that 'men are actually unaware of most of the things that they do . . .,' and 'since tendencies of which one has no awareness are not likely to be inhibited or redirected, unconscious behavior patterns tend to persist' (Shibutani, 1961 : 293). However, as Shibutani's discussion of the unconscious is very brief, eclectic in nature, and presented in a text for introductory social psychology students, it does not provide us with much of a basis for assessing interactionism's ability to provide a sound treatment of the unconscious. We find the basic criticism, that interactionism has failed to come to grips with the impact of the unconscious component in human behavior, to be a valid one.

Let us take up now the second major 'in-house' stricture, that one of interactionism's key concepts, self, is the source and object of much confusion and disagreement. It is possible to find in the writings of a single interactionist, Mead for example, definitions of self which are quite diverse in nature. On certain occasions an interactionist will speak of the I component of self, and on other occasions speak as if : (1) the self is solely a product of the uncritical incorporation of the opinion of others, and (2) the only component of self is the Me. Apparently, such shifting definitions are the product of their author's vacillations of position with respect to the extent that human behavior is determined. We do not, however, wish to convey the impression that the majority of present-day interactionists operate with confused and shifting conceptions of the self. Such does not seem to be the case.

Many, perhaps most, symbolic interactionists hold a clear and consistent definition of the concept self. The difficulty (and it is a matter of opinion whether it even constitutes a difficulty) arises because, while most present-day interactionists have firm and clearly stated conceptions of the self, no single conception is shared by this majority. In fact, such definitions as are shared by sizable factions of interactionists are not simple variants of one another but tend to stand in marked contrast. There are at least two different ways of conceiving 'self,' each of which holds the allegiance of a fairly large number of interactionists (Reynolds, et al., 1970 : 423). One of these conceptualizes the self as a multiple phenomenon and typically maintains that a person has as many selves as there are people about whose opinions he/she cares, or that a person has as many selves as there are groups in which he/she holds membership. The other basic conception of self sees it as a unitary phenomenon, a particular kind of process.

Now, as we previously indicated, whether or not such a disparity in the way a basic concept is defined constitutes a problem is a matter of opinion. Recent research indicates that how one defines the self is very much related to how one defines or conceives of such concepts and issues as social control, culture, socialization, social change, and methodology (Reynolds and McCart, 1972 : 35–9). Those who see the self as a multiple entity tend to: (1) equate social organization with culture, (2) define social control as control by others without reference to self-control, (3) define culture in functionalist terminology, (4) see both socialization and social change as merely processes by which members of *homo sapiens* are transformed into human beings, and (5) favor a methodological approach which combines empiricism with interpretative techniques. By contrast, those who view the self as a unitary entity tend to: (1) define both social organization and culture in nonfunctionalist, behavioral terms, (2) see social control as resting primarily on self-control, (3) define socialization as a process whereby individuals acquire those mechanisms which enable them to symbolically construct their environments, (4) see social change as a continuous process whereby people conjointly construct their lives rather than merely being acted upon by and responding to forces external to them, and (5) favor participant observation as a methodological tool.

These two divergent ways of conceiving of self—that is, as unitary or multiple entities—rest upon quite different images of both human beings and society and on equally divergent pictures of the assumed individual–society nexus. They are, in short, different varieties of sociological reasoning and, hence, different brands of symbolic interactionism. The extent to which one views the multiple self *versus* unitary self debate as a problem depends on his/her assessment of the relative merits of the more basic styles of sociological reasoning associated with each of these basic definitions. If one is convinced that the two styles are of equal or roughly equal worth, then the existence of these two disparate views on the nature of self obviously does not constitute much of a problem. On the other hand, if one holds that one of these styles of sociological reasoning is superior to the other, then the widespread existence of divergent definitions of the self does, indeed, constitute a problem of some magnitude. We favor that basic pattern of social psychological reasoning underlying the unitary conception of self. Yet, we do not accept it uncritically and *in toto*. Divergent definitions of self are, for us, somewhat of a problem; but, it is a problem that will not be solved until such time, if ever, as one brand of interactionist reasoning becomes the sole extant form of interactionist thought. For our part, we are not at all sure that such a gain in conceptual and theoretical closure would be worth the cost to be paid for it in terms of the loss of productive debate between the varieties of interactionism.

The last of the major 'inside' criticisms to be addressed, that the perspective is beset by numerous problems of a methodological nature, is the most frequently voiced of all the 'in-house' questionings. In many respects, this is perhaps the most difficult of all critical remarks to deal with in summary fashion. Again, we can do little here save to indicate our basic agreement with the statement that interactionism has its methodological problems. As we have previously noted, Mead nowhere detailed the methodological procedures to be associated with his perspective on human behavior. And Blumer's major statement on the nature of the perspective, according to Mullins (1973 : 30), offered no definition 'of research methods; thus, by implication, he defined symbolic interactionism as largely a way of thinking.'

Not only have most symbolic interactionists failed to produce systematic discussions of what they take to be a proper methodology, but what has come to be their most basic technique, participant observation, is itself a method which does not allow for much systematic exposition. Participant observation is a technique whose procedures are both difficult to spell out and equally difficult to teach or pass on to one's students. Furthermore, as Mullins points out, because participant-observation studies typically take a long time to complete, an adequate detailing of the exact methodological procedures one has employed during each step of an on-going investigation is difficult to report accurately. Most symbolic interactionists are not unaware of the more easily detailed survey research and experimental-design techniques employed in sociology; however, they consciously reject these techniques, opting instead for life-history and participant-observation techniques. These latter techniques, while admittedly most difficult to describe in systematic fashion, it is believed will ultimately provide a far more realistic picture of human conduct. In the meantime, the perspective remains fairly difficult to research, and it perhaps generates too few testable hypotheses. Nevertheless, these methodological problems do not appear to be insurmountable, as many interactionists continue to produce a reasonably large number of high quality studies. Furthermore, as we shall see later, the presumed failure to elaborate interactionism's verification procedures is not tantamount to neglecting to specify the perspective's methodology at all.

NON-INTERACTIONIST CRITICISMS

We shall deal with negative assessments of interactionists and interactionism by non-interactionists in the same manner as we have dealt with in-house, or reflexive, commentary; i.e. we shall compile what we take to be a representative list of such criticisms, holding our comments to a bare minimum while doing so; we shall then summarize and briefly comment on these criticisms; and, lastly, we shall discuss certain criticisms in some detail, offering assessments of their merits. As was the case with our treatment of self-critical remarks, the views to be dealt with here are those concerned primarily with contemporary symbolic interactionists. Those readers wishing to pursue non-interactionist critiques of both American pragmatism and early symbolic interactionism are referred to the writings of W. Williams (1966 : 402–5), H. K. Wells (1971), C. Lasch (1965 : Chapter V), and M. Natanson (1956 : 56–92).

A set of fairly representative 'outside' criticisms can be listed as follows:

1 Symbolic interactionism tends to be ahistorical and non-economic, especially in its approach to social problems. The particular phenomena or specific problems selected for study are only rarely linked to their historical origins and development (F. Block, 1973 : 39–41; D. L. Smith, 1973a; R. Ropers, 1973). This criticism has been voiced in the following manner (Smith, 1973a : 74–5):

> Symbolic interactionism as managed by the Loflands does not include social and historical conditions as relevant. . . . Focusing upon imputed definitions as autonomous from the social and historical conditions in which they exist results in a meaningless approach for people living in the closing decades of the twentieth century. . . . Social conditions, to be sure, are related to symbols and interaction [but they are also] related to the major institutions and their historical development.

This same basic criticism has also been directed at the social psychology of Mead : 'The activities that he sees men engaged in are not historically determined relationships of social and historical continuity; they are merely episodes, interactions, encounters, and situations' (Ropers, 1973 : 50).

2 The interactionist perspective has a limited view of the nature of social power. Symbolic interactionism is most useful in analyzing questions of social power under conditions of both low institutionalization and a roughly equal distribution of power when 'the outcomes of negotiations are to be explained'; but, 'Under other circumstances and when other issues are addressed, its utility is limited and its insight may even be biased' (Kanter, 1972 : 88).

3 Symbolic interactionism either ignores or has a faulty conception of social organization and social structure (Gouldner, 1970a: 379).

4 Symbolic interactionism presents too quaint and exotic a picture of social reality (Shaskolski, 1970, and Horowitz, 1971).

5 Symbolic interactionism is afflicted with certain ideological and philsophical biases which distort its picture of collective social life. In the words of one critic (Huber, 1973a: 275):

> the SI tradition shares with the philosophy of pragmatism from which it originates an epistemology which makes it reflect the social biases of the researcher and of the people whose behavior is observed. In a benignly liberal climate of opinion the outcome tends to go unnoticed; but in the long run, this kind of methodology is sensitive to the forces of social control.

6 Symbolic interactionism may be culturally and temporally limited in so far as it seems to apply best in those societies and situations where one habitually addresses himself/herself to the expectations of a multitude of different others (generalized others) rather than to those situations where one attempts to present the 'same self' on all or nearly all occasions. Interactionism may be more an accurate description of a 'new' personality type in the making, the 'other-directed' person, than it is a truly adequate account of the nature of human nature. The perspective appears at its very best in analyzing the fluid, noncommital encounter and at its very worst in analyzing the economically interested or emotionally binding relationship.

7 Ethnomethodology, if properly a variant of symbolic interactionism, is its least useful and most unsociological variety (Mayrl, 1973). The great appeal of ethnomethology to contemporary sociologists lies in the fact that its works appears to be concretely and immediately human. However, as W. W. Mayrl (1973:28) quickly points out,

> what is immediately human is not *fully* human. In fact, it is also ironic that while all social research must deal with abstractions, the ethnomethodologists, by focusing upon the consciousness of the solitary individual, have picked the one abstraction which is not justifiable. Unlike economic, political, religious and familial processes it cannot be concretized by being put back into a larger structural context of which it is a part.

The remainder of Mayrl's critique of ethnomethodology merits quotation in concluding our initial listing of the non-interactionist assessments of symbolic interactionism. Mayrl concludes his analysis with the following critical statement (1973 : 28):

> As Marx, Mead, and more recently, Goffman among many others have forcefully demonstrated, social relationships are derivable (and explainable) from social relationships and not individual consciousness. The only thing that can be derived from the solitary ego is the solitary ego.
>
> Social phenomenology, like all idealism, is an exercise in avoidance. The assumption of the priority of individual consciousness over history and the division of labor represents the feeble attempt to control these perplexing realities by substituting them for something which seems more manageable. Dreitzel is correct in pointing to fundamental similarities between the hippie movement and ethnomethodology. The former's response to crises in society is quite analogous to the latter's solution to problems in sociology.

Ethnomethodology, then, is subject to most of the criticisms applied both to other varieties of interactionism and to symbolic interactionism generally; i.e. it tends to be apolitical, ahistorical, and non-economic and to have, accordingly, faulty conceptions of social power and social organization. As we criticized ethnomethodology in chapter 2, we shall offer no further critique of it here.

We have listed several basic 'outsider' criticisms of interactionism—namely, that it is non-economic, ahistorical, culturally limited, and ideologically biased, has a limited view of social power, and paints an odd picture of social reality. These negative remarks are more applicable to ethnomethodology than to other orientations in symbolic interactionism. However, many of these comments collapse into, can easily be subsumed under, or are simply different manifestations of, a more general criticism which we also listed, namely, that symbolic interactionism lacks a proper appreciation of social organization and social structure. This, of course, is simply another way of stating that interactionism may have an astructural, or microscopic, bias; and a perspective with an astructural bias is one that by definition will tend to be non-economic, ahistorical, and with reference to power politics, apolitical. Hence, numerous thinkers working within the confines of such a perspective may well end up describing a social reality that is both preoccupied with the exotic and limited in transcultural applicability. In the light of this view, we feel that most of these criticisms can adequately be dealt with by directly discussing in detail what we have termed the astructural bias.

In addition to the charge of an astructural bias, there is one other listed criticism of some importance which we intend to discuss, namely, that symbolic interactionism suffers from certain other biases, some of which are ideological in nature. In the last analysis, the astructural and ideological biases may feed into and reinforce one another; indeed, the two are most difficult to separate, as the following discussion will reveal. After discussing these two interrelated, fundamental criticisms, we shall present our general assessment of their merits. This assessment, in turn, will serve to conclude this book.

INTERACTIONISM AND ITS BIASES

Any discussion of criticisms of the ideological biases of interactionism in commentaries on the perspective need not be lengthy, for such criticisms are few in number.[1] Just as Mead managed, for the most part, to escape scathing denouncements from those opposed to his social philosophy, so too, by and large, have contemporary symbolic interactionists. This may be so because, as Petras (1966) has suggested, symbolic interactionism has always 'fitted in' with the dominant orientation in American sociology. It is in this light that N. Mullins (1973:75) refers to interactionism as 'the loyal opposition.' Quite recently, this benign view of interactionism has begun to change. A small number of systematic and sustained critical analyses of the biases felt to be associated with the perspective have made their appearance in the sociological literature.

In spelling out interactionism's ideological biases and their attendant social consequences, the writings of four sociologists, Shaskolsky (1970), Lichtman (1970), Huber (1973a), and A. Gouldner (1970a) convey the gist of the sociological commentary embraced within the parameters of this category of criticism. Shaskolsky's remarks, which deal with symbolic interactionism in truly sweeping and, often-times, unwarranted generalities, are found in a single short article, and thus can be quickly detailed. The same situation holds for both Lichtman and Huber, although neither of them makes as sweeping an 'indictment.' On the other hand, the comments that Gouldner makes are not restricted to a single article, but are to be found in a major sociological treatise, an article, and a book review. Furthermore,

Gouldner does not deal with symbolic interactionism proper, but has chosen instead to aim his specific criticisms at major, although still representative, present-day spokespersons for the perspective. Although Gouldner seldom refers to interactionism in general, his criticisms of specific interactionists mark the beginnings of a truly systematic, sociological critique of the adequacy of symbolic interactionism as a perspective on human behavior.

We shall begin with those criticisms of Shaskolsky, Lichtman, and Huber which, in one way or another, deal with the general interactionist framework, and we shall then take up the far more specific comments of Gouldner. Along the way we shall also intersperse, where relevant, criticisms voiced by other non-interactionists.

Shaskolsky's brief overview of symbolic interactionism begins with the following statement: 'Symbolic interactionism has its roots deeply imbedded in the cultural environment of American life, and its interpretation of society is, in a sense, a "looking glass" image of what society purports to be' (1970:16). B. Malinowski (1944:53) once informed us that one should never expect to really understand a society or an institution by merely examining its charter. Shaskolsky, asserting that symbolic interactionism has uncritically accepted American society's conceptions of itself at their face value and has made them integral theoretical assumptions and conceptual constructs, argues that interactionism has become both a part of American society's charter and a variety of what J. Manis (1972) calls 'common sense sociology.' From Shaskolsky's vantage point, then, symbolic interactionism is merely an intellectual manifestation of American society's charter rather than a candid and accurate description of the larger features of the corporate state. Shaskolsky (1970:16) further argues that one negative consequence of what he takes to be interactionism's graphic representation and encapsulation of American values is that it is 'an ethnocentric factor which has vitiated . . . its adoption into the academic thinking of other countries.' We must interpolate an aside, however, to the effect that one could just as well argue that the adoption of symbolic interactionism into a social and cultural context differing from the American scene would lend it a specific critical dimension which Shaskolsky feels is now missing. In point of fact, the framework is finding favor in an increasing number of sociology departments at major European universities.

Shaskolsky proceeds with his critical remarks by noting that interactionism is a refined and realistic variety of social Darwinism. He argues that it is a form of social Darwinism incompatible with the 'robber baron' variety of *laissez faire* capitalism but quite compatible with and sympathetic to corporate capitalism's early phase of development. Shaskolsky (1970 : 17) puts the matter as follows :

> not for Mead a Sumnerian jungle society favoring the fittest, but a society undergoing gradual change and held together by the empathetic understanding of interacting individuals.

> In society, the rough-and-ready capitalism of the halcyon days of the 'robber barons' had been replaced by the philanthropic capitalism of their more sensitive descendants. The next step— welfare capitalism in the form of the New Deal legislation—was waiting offstage in history's wings. Symbolic interactionism reflected these subtle changes in American society.

While contending, on the one hand, that certain aspects of interactionism make it finely attuned to shifts in the structure of American society, Shaskolsky also argues that certain other facets of the perspective seem to make it 'oblivious to the true nature of society' (p. 19). It is in this latter context that Shaskolsky (1970 : 19–20) concludes his criticism of interactionism by raising the following disturbing question :

> What effect, for instance, does the fact of being a Negro have on the smooth interaction between individuals in 'defining the situation'—would the possession of a black skin be merely to add one further factor into those of which account must be taken when defining the situation, or would the color of the skin be the sole or at least the decisive factor in determining the performance of the individuals involved? In brief, can symbolic interactionism retain its validity in a society in which some men are more equal, or more free, than others?

In Shaskolsky's opinion, interactionism is wanting in this crucial respect. A similar argument is made by R. Lichtman (1970:75), when he observes that symbolic interactionism's principal weakness lies in its failure to unearth the true source(s) of actors' 'social constructions of reality' and 'definitions of the situation.' Lichtman argues that symbolic interactionists, by pretending to bracket the genetic question, implicitly assume that these definitions of the situation are either solely or primarily the result of actors' subjective constructs which, through the interaction process, add up to the construction of an additional intersubjective 'social' reality. Given the mass-media-engineered and -created definitions of our times, times in which some individuals are so situated that they command nearly instant access to millions of other actors' subjective realities with which to construct *the* definition of the situation, a quaint or 'unreal' air seems to float over the camp of symbolic interactionism.

It is this unreal aspect that Lichtman sees in symbolic interactionism that leads him to classify it as a variant of social idealism. He criticizes 'social idealism' in the following manner (1970 : 77):

> it is overly subjective and voluntaristic, lacks an awareness of historical concreteness, is naïve in its account of mutual typification and ultimately abandons the sense of human beings in a struggle against an alien reality which they both master and to which they are subordinate.

Lichtman then sets down, as follows, a series of criticisms which apply to symbolic interactionism as the least idealistic and most 'social' of all the varieties of 'social idealism' (1970 : 77–83):

1 Human action can neither be understood apart from or solely in terms of the interpretations of an actor. Recognition of the category of false consciousness is necessary for the understanding of social acts. Activity has an objective structure that is very often discrepant with its intended meaning.

2 The channeling of interpreted meanings is class-structured and is formed through lived engagements in the dominant institutions of society, which are class-dominated and bear a specific class structure.

3 If we are simply what we believe each other to be, the self-fulfilling prophecy becomes the major paradigm of social life; though this is true in some cases, it certainly is not in many others.

4 Human activities have a relationship to each other which is an objective constituent of the world. They exist whether they are a part of our subjectivity or not.

This same 'unreal quality' catches the attention of I. Horowitz (1971 : 527), who singles it out in discussing the work of the prominent Chicago school interactionist H. S. Becker:

> the amount of mechanical activity and behavioral response to organizational pressures and institutional constraints is either left out or reinterpreted into terms more amenable to personality, i.e.

family problems, etc. In short, the philosophical bias of . . . voluntarism may create a more 'wide open' and hence more exotic (albeit 'deviant') universe, than the one people live in every day.

Shaskolsky, Lichtman, and Horowitz, then, all see in symbolic interactionism a quality of unreality, which they feel stems from either the specific biases associated with voluntarism or the larger set of biases associated with social idealism, a philosophical system which usually contains voluntarism itself as one of its key elements. It was with reference to this particular bias that Shaskolsky has remarked that interactionism's picture of the social world is a utopia which happens to be written in the present tense.

Let us turn now to J. Huber's analysis of the biases of symbolic interactionism, or, as she terms it, the bias of emergent theory.[2] Huber (1973a : 274) begins her critique by noting that J. Lofland, H. Becker, and S. Bruyn have all, in one fashion or another, observed that the perspective has not really been clearly formulated, that its theoretical postulates and methodology are not systematically articulated, that its specific instructions on how one does qualitative observation and analysis are sparse, and that its directives as to how one is to convince others of the validity of one's results are non-existent. Huber (1973a : 276) goes on to note that both Meltzer and E. Stevens have also observed that many of the printed works from which initial knowledge of the framework derived were not originally intended for publication and had to be posthumously published. The upshot of the foregoing observations is that the relationship between theory and method remains unclear in the writings of most symbolic interactionists. And this brings Huber to her basic criticism of interactionism, which she puts in the following words (1973a : 276):

> When the place of theory is unclear, when the theoretical expectations are not explicated, then the social givens of the present serve as an implicit theoretical formulation. . . .All of these formulations have a *status quo* bias for, when no theoretical expectations are specified, and when truth is expected to emerge from interaction, then what is taken to be true tends to reflect the distribution of social power among the participants.

In part, this paucity of theoretical formulation which occasions a *status quo* bias results from that domain assumption of American pragmatism which dictates that truth is created rather than discovered in practice. When such an assumption is in force, the best theory is taken to be that 'grounded type' which emerges from direct observation, particularly if that observation is of a participatory nature. Under such circumstances, there will be little interest in spelling out beforehand the exact rules of logic and procedures to be employed in theory construction. And, as Huber (1973a : 281) informs us :

> When the theoretical formulation is primitive, when it 'emerges' from the research, or when it is absent, then investigators will tend to use implicitly their own social givens as a theory. When the subjects studied by the sociologists participate in the formulation of emerging theory, their own givens are added to the emerging theory.

The fact that this emergent bias has not been an obvious one derives, in turn, from the specific types of people frequently investigated by symbolic interactionists; for their subjects have been people who possess little or no real social power. Because these subjects have so little power, 'any lack of consensus among the participants in such situations can be settled by the researcher with little backtalk from the participants' (1973a : 281). Were the typical subjects of the interactionist's research representatives of either a more powerful class or at least more powerful groups, the presence of the emergent bias, Huber feels, would be manifestly obvious. Her reasoning on this point can be seen in the following statement (1973a : 281–2) :

> The problem of scientific objectivity raised by lack of a prior theoretical formulation, by the absence of clearcut criteria for selecting creditable informants, would be highlighted were the researcher to inspect a group of topdogs, say, the executives of a major corporation. In this situation, the researcher's colleagues might be uneasy if the researcher could not distinguish between theoretical concepts and observed behavior, if the hierarchy of credibility of the informants were arbitrary, and if other such judgmental procedures could hardly be replicated. Which of the participants in an interactive setting is to have most influence in determining the shape of an emerging theory is a question that the SI model has not confronted. . . . Nothing prevents a detailed observational account from being informed with notions from a stratification theory or any other theory. For the researcher to spell out in

advance and in detail what is expected is more work than trans-
scribing events with the atheoretical simplicity of a blank mind.
But such preliminary spadework would help to integrate the findings into a larger body of work, and hence make them more meaningful.

According to Huber, there is good reason for one to spell out one's
logically-related theoretical propositions in advance of his/her research endeavours, because to do so forces the researcher both to predict a specific set of results and to explain why such results should
logically be recorded. Failure to detail these theoretical propositions
results in a situation where the symbolic interactionist always wins,
for failure to bet on a specific outcome makes any and all outcomes
permissible. This is a curious observation on Huber's part, for she
has just argued with some success that in the absence of an explicitly
stated theory and method the social givens of participant and researcher alike come to constitute the theoretical framework and, in so
doing, give the associated research 'a bias which reflects the unstated
assumptions of the researcher, the climate of opinion in the discipline,
and the distribution of power in the interactive setting' (1973a : 282).
Surely, the biases of the researcher and of the society of which he/she
is a part always lead him/her to bet on some outcomes more than
others. Otherwise why would Huber herself be so concerned with
the emergent bias among interactionists?
  Huber's main criticism, then, is not so much that interactionism
fails to predict the expected outcomes of its research, but that interactionism suffers from a propensity which prevents it from coming
to grips with such larger problems as social stratification and social
power. In short, an emergent bias gives rise to an astructural bias.
  We move now to a brief discussion of the highly specific criticisms
of Gouldner, who delivers an assessment of social causes and political consequences of the 'definitions of the situation' constructed by
Goffman and Becker, two of America's leading symbolic interactionists.
  Gouldner embarks upon his critical analysis of Goffman's 'all the
world's a stage and life's but a theater' approach to human behavior
with the observation that Goffman's work displays an astructural
bias. In Gouldner's (1970a : 379) terms, 'it [Goffman's theory] is a
social theory that dwells upon the episodic and sees life only as it is
lived in a narrow interpersonal circumference, ahistorical and non-

institutional, an existence beyond history and society, and one which comes alive only in the fluid, transient "encounter".' Political consequences attach to such a conception of human nature and the social order (1970a : 379):

> Goffman's rejection of hierarchy often expresses itself as an *avoidance* of social stratification and of the importance of power differences, even for concerns that are central to him; thus, it entails an accommodation to existent power arrangements.

The point Gouldner is making here is a frequently-voiced and quite elementary one; ignoring the structure simply aids in its perpetuation. Goffman then, rather than having a generic theory of human selfhood and behavior, has a theory whose appeal is restricted to people caught in the throes of a seemingly inflexible bureaucratic structure whose ultimate victory over them, they, as does Goffman apparently, readily, if not eagerly, concede. Goffman's dramaturgical variant on symbolic interactionism deals primarily with those secondary adjustments which people make to 'the overpowering social structures that they feel must be taken as given' (1970a : 382). In a quite different context, which no longer appears as different as it formerly did, Gouldner (1961) once noted how quickly sociologists accept the domination of the bureaucracy over men and women. And, rather than enlightening people as to how the bureaucracy can be not only bested but dismantled, they become eager morticians of the human aspirations, hopes, and dreams which the bureaucracy has managed to crush. Not everyone, however, appears to applaud Goffman's cleverly-staged presentation of a social psychological theory. For, as Gouldner informs us, 'a dramaturgical model is an accommodation congenial only to those who are willing to accept the basic allocations of existent master institutions, for it is an invitation to a "side game" ' (1970a : 386).

If it is indeed a side game, the question becomes : whose game is it, and is it the only game in town? Gouldner appears to answer this question when he observes that, in the world of Goffman, value does not depend upon substance but upon style. The value of human beings lies not in their energies, abilities, or even good works, but in mere appearances. Apparently, Goffman's world is not the world of the Protestant Ethic character, the old, or classical, bourgeois. However, by Gouldner's reasoning, Goffman's theory has not totally abandoned the world of the bourgeois but merely 'entered deep into the world of the new bourgeois.' In fact, 'Goffman's dramaturgy is an obituary for the old bourgeois virtues and a celebration of the new ones' (1970a:381 and 383). Not only this new world is reflected in Goffman's model; so, too, are the interests of that new middle class which no longer subscribes to the Protestant Ethic dictate of success via hard work. As Gouldner points out, 'there is a keen sense of the irrationality of the relationship between individual achievement and the magnitude of reward, between actual contribution and social reputation' (1970a:381).

There is, then, in Goffman's writings an implicit, yet important, distinction being made, that between production (of symbols and values, as well as other 'social products') and exchange as social functions. Furthermore, Goffman apparently recognizes, at least implicitly, that people are rewarded by their contribution not to production but to exchange. Goffman appears to be applauding this state of affairs. *The Presentation of Self in Everyday Life* is a new and reverse doctrine of utilitarianism. Goffman and his fellow dramaturgical interactionists are twentieth-century J. Benthams, arguing in defense of the natural right, nay, the duty, to deceive one's neighbor.

Human beings are both bought and sold, and indeed must sell (package?) themselves on the market (stage?). Goffman's framework imputes this state of affairs to a natural 'order of things' and accommodates itself accordingly. If one reads closely enough, Goffman is telling actors how to become smashing successes within the structure of the bureaucracy. This work is a semi-sociological *Rules of Order* for uptight petty bureaucrats; it is an organization man's Bible, the new Horatio Alger story, a social psychological Dale Carnegie course. We are being invited by the proponents of the dramaturgical model to come on stage, enter the play, join the game, and live in life's cracks, or niches, as we find and define them. According to Gouldner, this dramaturgical model 'invites us to carve a slice out of time, history, and society, rather than to attempt to organize and make manageable the larger whole' (1970a:385). In short, the dramaturgical genre of symbolic interactionist Goffman beseeches us to act 'natural,' to deceive both self and others while paying homage to the great bureaucracy, that omnipotent God of things-as-they-are-now.

In closing this brief discussion of Gouldner's critique of Goffman, one point of criticism deserves additional emphasis. The point is simply this: Goffman always 'fails to be explicit in his commitment to the bureaucratic model and all that such a model entails' (Fletcher, *et al.*, 1974:16). But one of the things that such a model entails is that it is essentially non-changing. As Fletcher and his associates have pointed out, 'Goffman's organization lacks a dynamic that would allow for, or bring about, change. While the organization has the power to transform selves, it is apparently unaffected by those persons who constitute its human fabric' (1974:18). This model of bureaucracy is precisely what channels Goffman into his overriding concern with mere 'secondary adjustments.' This bureaucracy is not capable of being beaten and dismantled, and his human beings are not the types of people who could do it even if it were possible. We mention Goffman's model of bureaucracy here because it, more than his dramaturgical metaphor, serves to set him and other dramaturgists apart from the main thrust of the symbolic interaction framework. Goffman avoids dealing with social stratification and social class inasmuch as he takes them as immutable givens. They are fixed and unchanging; and, hence, their influence is a constant. Consequently, Goffman's social psychology leads him into becoming totally absorbed by the secondary adjustments people make to such structures. He is concerned with a limited, game-playing variety of human behavior, which he mistakenly takes to be the full range of behavioral possibilities. Goffman's microsociological bias, then, is of a different nature from the astructural bias that reveals itself in the work of other interactionists. For example, such interactionists as A. Strauss and his associates (Strauss, 1963), holding an image of both society in general and the mental hospital in particular as 'negotiated orders,' become so preoccupied with people as the active creators of society that they sometimes lose sight of what Durkheim once termed the 'coerciveness of social life.' Unlike Goffman, they do not regard social organization and social structure as constant, unalterable influences, but rather they occasionally appear to assume that structural variables exert either minimal influence or none at all. Most symbolic interactionists are closer to Strauss in this respect than they are to Goffman. Theirs is a different type of microscopic bias, but it is a bias nonetheless.

Let us move on now to Gouldner's specific criticisms of Becker. With the possible exception of interactionism's Iowa school, few symbolic interactionists have been smitten with the fairy tale of *Wertfreiheit* sociology; indeed they do not even pay lip service to it. Most symbolic interactionists are value-committed, not value-free. Becker is no exception to this general trend. In fact, his work epitomizes the value-commited posture. Becker argues, and forcefully, not only that sociologists should be value-committed, but that their value commitment (and hence their sociology) should be to some specific group, category, or stratum. The specific category to which Becker and other Chicago school symbolic interactionists commit themselves is society's underdogs, those at the bottom of the social heap.

What Gouldner is objecting to, however, is that Becker, and a host of other interactionists, have singled out a very specific type of underdog to whom to profess their allegiance, namely, those underdogs who are, in a sense, already defeated. These include prison inmates, sexual nonconformists, petty criminals, mental patients, and what N. Polsky once called *Hustlers, Beats and Others* (1966). These are people to whom L. Dexter's (1962 : 226) remarks seem to apply when he informs us that it is the cheat and thief who truly admit the ultimate validity of the system by virtue of their short-cut method of conforming to it. Many in this group differ from members of the surrounding society only in the one respect of some specific deviation, and, apart from this, apparently 'go along' with the general system. For example, in their ranks are those members of the homosexual community who, in matters other than their sexual nonconformity, wear what L. Humphreys (1970 : 131–148) has called the 'breast plate of righteousness.'

Those underdogs who elicit the ostensible support of Becker's type of symbolic interactionist pose no real threat to the current structure of American society and its 'establishment.' But, while this class of underdogs presumably has its interests looked after by Becker and others, another class of underdogs remains ignored and unchampioned. Which of the Becker-style interactionists openly and actively side with the Black Panther type of underdog, who is not a 'beat' but beaten up and yet not beaten? Who sides with these underdogs, who fight back and whose very presence poses a threat to the current American establishment?

If one is to take sides, as H. Becker and a host of other interactionists would have us do, one must remember that to stand for someone is also, in many cases, to stand against someone. Numerous symbolic interactionists, in siding with Becker's type of underdog, stand against petty bureaucrats and the local caretakers of prisons and mental institutions. Gouldner seems to be asking: Who, among the symbolic interactionists, not only stands with the threatening, *status-quo*-challenging underdog but also forcefully stands against something more formidable than local caretakers and petty bureaucrats? Who stands against the National Institute of Mental Health, the topdog bureaucrats in the federal government, and the ruling class? If this were not criticism enough, one could just as readily question the degree to which the commitments of certain interactionists to the underdogs they strive to support are actually in the best interests of those underdogs. Indeed, this is exactly the point Gouldner (1970b) has argued in another context, and it bears repeating here. Gouldner, in the course of reviewing a book authored by prominent members of the American sociological establishment and endorsed by 'official' sociology, implicitly poses the question of just whose side certain interactionists are really on. In examining the book, Gouldner (1970b: 334) observes that it 'reflects the development of an important new alliance within sociology itself: between the old style Chicago-type participant observers and the . . . high science researchers.' This, in Gouldner's opinion, is the real 'political meaning of the book's genuflections toward Becker and Goffman, toward participant observation, and toward the Chicago school more generally' (1970b: 334).

Gouldner contends that this new coming together of symbolic interactionism and structural functionalism is, in part, based on 'the Welfare State's need for more Chicago-type informal research techniques, particularly when studying illicit or illegal behavior' (1970b: 334). He further argues that 'the new alliance reflects the utility of "informal" research methods, and the helplessness of survey and experimental techniques, for the Welfare State's internal domestic, counter insurgency programs' (1970b: 334). While cautioning here against what may be a mistaken tendency to equate participant observation and symbolic interactionism (a price to be paid by interactionism for its failure to systèmatically spell out its methodology), let us elaborate upon Gouldner's discussion of the 'new interactionist-functional alliance,' as it will bring us around again to the question of whose side some interactionists are really on.

Structural functionalism, that curious mixture of mild liberalism and ultra-conservatism which has served so well the interests of the social system in the past, now needs its basic conservatism reworked and remolded if it is to meet the new needs of the welfare-warfare state. A seemingly simple tactic, possibly enabling sociological conservatism to carry the day, would be to take on a liberal ally, namely, the symbolic interactionist. Gouldner appears to think that the sociological establishment already has its new ally well in tow. He sees the interactionists and functionalists, arm in arm with functionalism's old allies, the social action theorists, marching to the cadence set by the welfare state's new requirements. A similar point is made in the following statement (Nicolaus, 1970 : 274–8) : [3]

Sociologists (read structural functionalists here) stand guard in the garrison and report to its masters on the movements of an occupied populace. The more adventurous sociologists (read symbolic interactionists here) don the disguise of the people and go out to mix with the peasants in the 'field,' returning with the books and articles that break the protective secrecy in which a subjugated population wraps itself, and make it more accessible to manipulation and control.

This is precisely what we meant earlier when we suggested that, perhaps, Becker's style of interactionist does no real favor for those underdogs with whom he does attempt to side. It was in reference to this exact point that Smith (1973b : 158) has remarked that many interactionists are 'mod squad' types.

The allegation that symbolic interactionism has become, or is in the process of becoming, part of American sociology's *status quo* springs primarily from the camp of critical sociology; however, such a charge finds some support from what, less than a decade ago, would have seemed a most unlikely quarter. Consider the following 'modest' statement by T. Parsons (1964 : 150) :

Here it is first to be said the explicit concern with general theory has been confined to a relatively small number of persons, most notably myself and a small number closely associated with me at some stage of their careers. However, stemming mainly from the same roots, partly through direct association, the work of Merton and his students is closely related. This does not, however, by any means mean that the underlying influence of such earlier movements as that of the 'social psychology' of C. H. Cooley, G. H. Mead, and W. I. Thomas has ceased to be important. Indeed it has fitted in closely with the more structural-functional movement.

Many of the foregoing criticisms of the ideological and implicit biases of both symbolic interactionism in general and specific interactionists, as diverse as they are, share at least one major point in common. In noting that symbolic interactionism seems oblivious to the real nature of human society (Shaskolsky 1970:19), that it may picture a more open world than the one people actually live in (Horowitz, 1971:524), and that it focuses upon the episodic (Gouldner, 1970a:379), these comments imply that symbolic interactionism lacks a proper appreciation or adequate conception of social organization. It is quite reasonable to suggest that if one does not have social organization clearly in focus, or, worse yet, has no conception of social organization at all, he/she is intellectually prevented both from coming to grips with society's dominant, or master, institutions and from formulating an adequate account of human social life. As we find this to be the most damaging of all the criticisms leveled at interactionism, it is not enough to simply assert the existence of such an astructural bias. Neither, of course, will it suffice merely to illustrate its presence in the works of a small number of interactionists no matter how prominent they may be. Rather, if Shaskolsky's, Lichtman's, Huber's, Horowitz's, Gouldner's, and others' criticisms are to be given serious attention, then it must be demonstrated that this microsociological bias is truly widespread among contemporary representatives of the interactionist paradigm. A comprehensive survey of the matter would exceed the scope of this portion of our book. However, we shall provide some evidence that will allow us to make a tentative assessment.

THE ASTRUCTURAL BIAS: RECENT EVIDENCE

Fortunately, as a result of some fairly recent research on the varieties of symbolic interactionism, we are in a position to examine the conceptions of social organization subscribed to by modern interactionists. As part of a larger study of theoretical diversity among interactionists, Reynolds (1969; 1970; 1972; 1973) constructed and mailed a questionnaire to 124 sociologists closely associated with the symbolic interactionist perspective.[4] Eighty-four of these sociologists completed and returned the questionnaire, and hence constitute the sample of interactionists to whom the following remarks clearly apply.

These interactionists were offered a set of four alternative definitions of social organization, all direct quotations from the symbolic interaction literature, and were asked to select the one definition that most closely approximated to their own working conception. If no quotation offered matched or approximated the respondent's own definition, he/she was encouraged to write in a personal definition of what social organization was 'all about.' In addition, each respondent was asked to list, in order of importance, what he/she considered to be the most indispensable concepts for sociological reasoning.

Reynolds (1969:71) presented respondents with the following definitions of social organization:

1 Social organization: (a) the structure of common meanings and values of a society (since meanings and values are often structured into institutions, the social organization is the totality of institutions), (b) a condition of society in which the members have most of their meanings in common.

2 The term 'social organization' refers to a social relation in which the individuals so behave as to prevent the disruption of their mutual influences by extraneous events.

3 From a structural point of view, the framework of social organization consists in the members of the group and their cultural relationships. While the introduction of any new culture trait produces problems of readjustment and disorganization, it is also true that social organization is a result of cultural integration. That is, the attitudes, the folkways, mores, laws, and institutions make up a system of social controls which the group imposes on its members. In a sense, the social structure seems to be synonymous with culture, since culture affects the framework of social organization. On the other hand, social organization is at once the product of the total culture and a part of it, rather than the sum total of man's achievements.

4 The unity of the social mind consists not in agreement but in organization, in the fact of reciprocal influence or causation among its parts, by virtue of which everything that takes place in it is connected with everything else, and so is an outcome of the whole . . . this differentiated unity of mental and social life, present in the simplest intercourse but capable of infinite growth and adaptation, is what I mean by social organization.[5]

Before reporting the findings, a few words need to be said about the definitions themselves. Definition number 1 conceives of social organization as a system or condition of shared values and meanings. It should be immediately noted that this, obviously, is how the concept culture is defined by many, perhaps a majority, of sociologists. Definition number 3 goes so far as to explicitly equate culture with social organization, on the one hand, and to argue that social organization is simply a part of culture, on the other. Even when the term 'social organization' is linked to the word 'relationship' in definition 3, the relationship in question is a cultural, not a social, relationship. We should mention in passing here that considering culture and social organization as equivalents constitutes a pronounced tendency among structural functionalists. Functionalists frequently deal with the 'cultural system' while referring to it as the 'social system.' A glance at definition 4 reveals that it, too, appears to confuse culture with organization by adding a mentalistic component to its conception of social organization, speaking of 'mental life' and 'the social mind.' Definitions 1, 3, and 4, while somewhat wanting as definitions of culture, come much closer to being adequate definitions of culture than of social organization.

A different case is presented by definition 2. It can quite readily be argued that a reasonably useful conception of social organization views it as the principal, characteristic, or most important way in which people are related to people, or as the principal, or characteristic, form of human relationship. By way of illustration, and employing the above definition, one would note that the basic form of social organization in western Europe and North America is the short-term, depersonalized, atomistic contract, or, put more simply, the contractual relationship. Of the four definitions presented in Reynolds' questionnaire, only definition 2 deals with social organization as human or social relationships rather than as mental states or cultural values and beliefs. Hence, only definition 2 would appear to reveal a somewhat adequate appreciation of social organization.

The eighty-four symbolic interactionists in Reynolds' sample responded to these four alternatives in the following manner: three subjects failed either to select one of the alternatives or to write in a definition of their own choosing; sixty-four interactionists selected from among the four alternatives offered; seventeen respondents chose to provide their own definitions. Of the sixty-four respondents finding a listed definition to their liking, only six selected definition 2, the only definition among the four alternatives that deals with social organization in social rather than cultural terms. Thus, fifty-eight interactionists preferred definitions which reveal an astructural bias; that is, they do not consider human relationships to be central to their conceptions of social organization.

As we previously noted, seventeen interactionists rejected all four alternatives offered and elected instead to write in their own personal definitions of social organization. A content analysis of these write-in definitions revealed them to be somewhat diverse. Nine of these definitions turned out to be merely restatements, different ways of phrasing, or slightly modified versions, of definitions 1, 3, and 4. Hence, we may say that these interactionists, too, were prone to define social organization in the same manner in which culture tends to be defined, i.e. as a system or condition of shared values, beliefs, meanings, or expectations. However, eight of the seventeen subjects did offer definitions not dissimilar to definition 2. That is, in one way or another, this small set of symbolic interactionists saw social organization as involving, above all else, human relations or relationships. They tended to refer to social organization as the totality of binding relations, patterned sets of relationships, or structured relationships. Human relationships were clearly at the center of the definitions provided by this very small number of interactionists. It is important to note that, of the thirty-one respondents in Reynolds' sample who received Ph.D.s from the University of Chicago, only one chose to write in a personal definition of social organization. This particular respondent did view social organization as directly concerned with human relationships, but he was only one of just four Chicago Ph.D.s who accepted this conception.

In sum, the findings from Reynolds' study reveal that a large majority of the symbolic interactionists in his sample lack an appreciation of social organization, either confusing it with culture or subsuming it under the larger rubric of culture as simply 'one of culture's parts.' In Reynolds' sample, this tendency is most pronounced among those interactionists who have received their training from, and/or served on, the sociology faculty at the University of Chicago. As Gouldner, Huber, Smith, and Horowitz appear to direct most of their critical comments at the Chicago school of symbolic interactionism, Reynolds suggests that their criticisms are not without foundation. If Reynolds' sample is at all representative, there is a pronounced antimacroscopic tendency among present-day interactionists; and replies to his request for a listing of 'indispensable concepts' further bear this out.

INTERACTIONISTS' INDISPENSABLE CONCEPTS

We previously noted that Reynolds asked his respondents to provide a list of those concepts which they felt were indispensable for sound sociological reasoning. As only seven numbered spaces were provided, respondents were limited as to the total number of concepts which could be listed. The average number of concepts cited was five; hence let us see which five concepts were most frequently listed and by how many symbolic interactionists.

The concept 'role' was the most frequently cited concept, being listed by thirty-eight respondents. The concepts 'self' and 'interaction' were each mentioned by thirty-seven interactionists. Twenty-nine respondents listed 'culture' as an indispensable concept, and twenty-five listed the concept 'norm.'

Of these five most frequently listed concepts, the first three (role, self, and interaction) are very closely associated with the perspective of symbolic interactionism. The remaining two concepts, culture and norm, are identified with structural functionalism. None of these five concepts mirrors a structural view of human social life. Furthermore, concepts usually identified with theorists who manifest interest in society's larger features received little mention by Reynolds' sample. For example, the concepts 'power' and 'social class' were listed by only two respondents. Only six subjects bothered to list the concept 'conflict.' Most importantly, the concept 'relationship,' or 'human relationship,' was indicated by only three interactionists. On the other hand, those concepts typically associated with a more individualistic view of society were cited with greater frequency. For example, seventeen interactionists listed 'socialization,' eight listed 'group,' and seven listed 'symbol.'

Evidently, the criticism that modern symbolic interactionism's microsociological concerns blind it to macrosociological matters has a measure of validity. Whether or not such a bias is necessarily inherent in the symbolic interactionist perspective remains to be seen.

A FINAL COMMENT

It will be recalled that the most basic 'in-house' criticisms of the perspective contend that interactionism has failed to elaborate its methodology systematically, has ignored emotions and the unconscious, and has failed to achieve anything approaching consensus on how the pivotal concept 'self' is properly defined. We have noted that we find ourselves in agreement with the basic thrust of these comments. We have agreed, for example, that interactionism has either ignored or renounced the idea of 'the unconscious' and has provided no explanatory principle in its place. We likewise have found ourselves agreeing with the charge that interactionism has tended to ignore many human emotions. However, we have pointed out that, while such affective phenomena as love and hate have been slighted, certain interactionists have dealt with phenomena like shame and embarrassment. Furthermore, we also noted that earlier interactionists tended to deal with numerous emotions.

We have agreed that the critics are precisely right in their observation that the concept 'self' is the object of much dissensus among interactionists. We have also stated that we regard this as a problem only because of our conviction that a definition of self that denotes a unitary phenomenon is far preferable to one which conceives the self as a multiple entity. On the other hand, we have also reasoned that the presence of competing conceptions of the self has led to productive debate on the part of interactionists. Such debate has been too productive to be terminated by any attempt at achieving premature closure in terms of how the paradigm's basic concepts must be defined.

In listing interactionists' criticisms of their own methodology, we have indicated our agreement that the perspective has generated relatively few testable hypotheses, that its concepts are hard to operationalize, and that its methods of observation are difficult to teach and replicate. However, we believe that one stricture against interactionism, that it has failed to spell out its methodology, is somewhat misplaced. When 'in-house' critics, such as Kuhn, make this criticism, what they really mean, we would claim, is that symbolic interactionism has failed to detail that portion of its total methodology which is concerned with verification procedures. As a perspective's methodology must be concerned both with its 'logic of discovery, or inquiry,' and with its procedures for verification, the charge that interactionism has not spelled out its methodology needs to be modified. Blumer (1969), after all, has expounded that part of symbolic interactionism's methodology which pertains to its overall logic of discovery, and Denzin has recently produced both a text and a reader on sociological methods. An appropriate criticism, therefore, would be that symbolic interactionism has largely failed to set down systematically what it considers the proper and precise procedures of verification to be utilized in researching the framework.

Unlike the 'in-house' critiques, the non-interactionists' criticisms, while appearing to be more diverse on the surface, tend to coalesce into a single major criticism. This criticism, as we have seen, concerns the micro-level character of the perspective.

We have agreed that the works of a great many symbolic interactionists are apolitical, non-economic, and ahistorical. Furthermore, most of these works are culturally limited. We do not, however, subscribe to the notion that such tendencies are inherent in the interactionist framework itself. Neither do we believe that interactionism is, of necessity, culturally limited and hopelessly microscopic. While it is true, for example, that interactionists have written little on political processes and structures, P. Hall has already taken steps to remedy this deficiency with his recent publication, 'A Symbolic Interactionist Theory of Politics.' Hall's work, as we have noted, suffers from a number of shortcomings, but it is nevertheless a worthwhile endeavor of the type needed to help offset the current apoliticality of interactionists. Similarly, the work of R. Brooks (1969) on a symbolic interactionist approach to political ideology should help stimulate interactionists' interest in political phenomena. Another interactionist work that attempts to deal with political and economic phenomena is A. Rose's *The Power Structure* (1967). It should be pointed out, however, that at those very points where Rose attempts to go macroscopic he approaches abandonment of his interactionist stance.

There is little in the way of rejoinder we can offer to the very telling allegation that symbolic interactionism has been ahistorical; for, indeed it has. The one instance we know of an interactionist work that not only locates its subject squarely within its historical context but also demonstrates the direct impact of history upon that subject is F. Merrill's (1961) study in the sociology of literature. The only interactionist manuscript specifically devoted to economics is the C. A. Hickman and M. H. Kuhn book, *Individuals, Groups, and Economic Behavior* (1956). It is far easier to respond to the charge that the interaction perspective is culturally limited. A number of interactionist studies of self-acquisition, self-conception, and socialization in differing cultural contexts have been done. Three such studies are Kuhn's essay on personality in Amish society (1954), Boogs' investigation of socialization among the Ojibwa (1956), and Driver's article on self-conception in India (1969). The number of investigations employing a symbolic interactionist perspective in cross-cultural context, however, has been rather small. Clearly, more such studies are needed, and so are additional interactionist examinations of macroscopic structures and processes. It should be noted, finally, that a fairly sizeable number of such studies have been undertaken by symbolic interactionists. Shibutani and K. M. Kwan have dealt with ethnic stratification (1965), R. Turner and L. Killian with collective behavior (1957), E. C. Hughes with the world of work (1958), M. Dalton with formal organization (1959), and D. Cressey with organized crime (1969).

Of all the presumed deficiencies of the symbolic interactionist paradigm, then, two stand forth as the most crucial: (1) limited consideration of human emotions, and (2) unconcern with social structure. In effect, the first of these shortcomings implies that symbolic interactionism is not psychological enough, while the second implies that symbolic interactionism is not sociological enough. Symbolic interactionism is, of course, a social psychological perspective; hence, it could be argued plausibly that what others consider limitations are seen by social psychologists as simply affirmations of the proper concerns of social psychology. We could let the matter rest there; but, of course, we shall not. Symbolic interactionism does not make distinctions between macroscopic and microscopic levels of reality; nor does it argue that human emotions are too 'psychological' to warrant attention, or that social structure is too 'sociological' to bother with. On the contrary, we consider symbolic interactionism to be a general perspective on human behavior and social life; and, therefore, whatever influences that behavior or structures that social life is a proper object of concern. It is well past the time for symbolic interactionists to extend their analyses of sentiments, such as shame and embarrassment, to such affective phenomena as love, hate, and anger. It is also overdue for interactionists to begin dealing more fully and on a large scale with problems of economic, political, and historical import. One should expect no less from the perspective that claims, and rightly so, to be the most sociological of all the 'social psychologies.' It is our conviction that symbolic interactionism is capable of providing an adequate treatment of both human emotions and social structure. Until this is done, any defense of symbolic interactionism which argues, as we have, that the present shortcomings of the perspective are not constitutive of it will ring as hollow as R. K. Merton's denial that structural functionalism is inherently conservative. To date, the best statement in refutation of the astructural bias is Blumer's article, 'Society as Symbolic Interaction' (1962).

Although we have devoted a fairly large proportion of this volume to critical commentary, ours has been a predominantly sympathetic exposition of the symbolic interaction framework. For, in spite of its shortcomings, interactionism still commends itself to the sociologically oriented social psychologists. Why? The answer can probably be found in the following statement (Manis and Meltzer, 1972 : 577):

> symbolic interactionism clearly represents the most sociological of social psychologies. Adopting a distinctly sociological perspective, it directs attention to the social derivation of man's unique attributes; it represents mind and self as society in microcosm; it describes how the members of any human group develop and form a common world; it illuminates the character of human interaction by showing that human beings share one another's behavior instead of merely responding to each other's overt behavior; and, in numerous other ways, it implicates the individual with society and society with the individual.

Notes

1 THE GENESIS OF SYMBOLIC INTERACTIONISM

1 For the most part, the early American sociologists viewed the behavior of men and women in society as primarily of an individualistic nature, rather than a societal nature or an interactive nature. For a discussion of the differences between these three perspectives in terms of the role each plays in organizing one's theory of human behavior, see chapter 1 in Petras (1973b).

2 While this view was to be popularized through the later work of the economist T. Veblen, especially in *The Theory of the Leisure Class* (1899), the sociologist E. A. Ross dismissed the idea of studying non-rational sources of motivation as outside the interests of the social psychologist (1908 : 94–5).

3 Certainly, we do not mean to imply that W. James was the only source used in the derivation of pragmatic principles, or even that he was the major source (see for example Lewis, 1972; Mills, 1966). But James, at least as perceived by the early interactionists, disseminated pragmatism through a psychology of everyday living— through life in a changing socio-cultural environment—and, this is where the relevance of pragmatism lay (see also Konvitz and Kennedy, 1960 : 27–8). In 'A Morality for Americans' (1891), James wrote, 'The ethical philosopher, therefore, whenever he ventures to say which course of action is the best, is on no essentially different level from the common man' (1971 : 166–7). For a discussion of the role played by Peirce, Wright and Royce in the development of interactionism, see Lincourt and Hare (1973).

4 Throughout this work, the term 'Chicago school' is used to refer to the variant of the interactionist tradition which continues the classical Meadian tradition. Briefly, as opposed to the 'Iowa school,' the 'Chicago school' emphasizes process not structure, sympathetic introspection not attitude scales, indeterminacy and emergence not determinacy. A fuller discussion of these two schools, as well as other variants, is contained in a later section of this work. For the original

statement and a later discussion in the context of other schools, see
Meltzer and Petras (1970; 1973). For an overview of 'Chicago sociology'
with respect to the development of the discipline in America, see,
R. E. L. Faris (1964).

5 'Social behaviorism' was a term that Mead used to describe his own
approach to the study of human conduct. For the most part, the term
is used as synonymous with 'symbolic interactionism,' and that is the
way in which it will be used here. As far as we know, only one
set of authors (Tucker and Stoeckel, 1969) has defined the two as
variants of the larger tradition differentiating between the
interactionism of the 'Chicago school' and the social behaviorism of
Mead.

6 Of course, we do not wish to romanticize the interactionists' position,
and we shall discuss the ideological biases present in such an approach
in the final section of this work. An excellent critique can be found
in Huber (1973a). We would suggest that one reason the role of
emergence became emphasized to the extent found in the works of
the early interactionists was to avoid being attacked as socially
deterministic by those operating in the mainstream of early American
sociology from an individual-generated perspective.

7 Which, as mentioned earlier, provided an interesting contrast to the
approaches of Cooley and Mead, who tended to emphasize
cooperative tendencies because of their interests in the 'acquiring
mechanisms' of personality.

8 True to the individual-generated perspective which organized the
early works of Thomas, he would not have agreed, at that time, with
this statement. In 1900, he wrote 'The instincts of man are congenital;
the arts and industries are acquired by the race and must be learned
by the individual after birth. . . . Instinctive activities are pleasurable
and acquired habits irksome' (1900 : 762).

9 Evidently, the parallels between Thomas and Mead were not of a
direct nature. In a personal communication to one of the
authors (Petras), H. Blumer observed that Thomas seemed, for the
most part, unaware of Mead's theories on time, and that he '. . .
could not understand Mead,' September 11, 1968. A letter Thomas
wrote to L. L. Bernard in 1928 stated, in part (Baker, 1973 : 245) :
> You will notice that I have added the names of Mead and Cooley
> to those who influenced me. I have preferred to say nothing
> about Dewey. When he came to the University, I was already
> offering a course in Social Origins. I gave him materials used in his
> address as President of the Philosophical Society about that time
> and it would be more correct to say that he came under my
> influence than that I came under his. It is true that I was interested

in his thought and certainly tried to use some of it in my classes, but Dewey has always seemed to me to be something of a mystic and a metaphysician and I found—or thought I found—that I was repudiating almost everything he said, or ignoring it. It may be, nevertheless, that he had more influence on me than I can remember. The same of Mead. [Author's note: This sentence was inserted in ink after the letter had been typed.] I am saying this to you by way of explanation and as a private matter.

10 And then, as A. Strauss (1964:xiii) has noted, with only the section on self. Sociologists have ignored the concepts entailed in Mead's philosophy of the present and the notions of emergence and sociality, even though these provide the framework within which the more sociological material is developed. While all who label themselves symbolic interactionists make a bow in the direction of Mead and his theories, many of the contemporary variants bear little resemblance to his own approach with respect to the context out of which individual and social behavior emerge.

2   VARIETIES OF SYMBOLIC INTERACTIONISM

1 This section draws heavily upon Meltzer and Petras (1970).
2 C. Tucker (1966:354-5). Tucker also points out that the TST contradicts its own purported assumptions by requiring the investigator to impose his own meanings on the subject's responses.
3 This section, as well as the two subsequent ones, draws upon Petras and Meltzer (1973).
4 See Mullins (1973:183-92) for a more complete discussion of Garfinkel's intellectual antecedents, co-workers, and students.

3   CRITICISMS OF SYMBOLIC INTERACTIONISM

1 This brief analysis of the astructural bias among present-day symbolic interactionists draws heavily upon a recent article by J. M. Reynolds and L. T. Reynolds, 'Interactionism, Complicity and the Astructural Bias.' *Catalyst*, 7, (Winter, 1973: 76-85).
2 See the interesting and sometimes acrimonious exchange over these comments between Blumer and Huber (Blumer, 1973: 797-8; Huber, 1973b:798-800).
3 Bracketed words supplied by present authors.
4 As there is no known universe of symbolic interactionists from which to draw a random sample, Reynolds selected his potential

respondents in the following manner : (1) the 31 symbolic interactionists who were in the 'pilot study' for the major investigation
were listed; (2) a panel composed of symbolic interactionists provided a
list of sociologists they considered to be closely associated with the
interactionist framework; (3) the authors of both major manuscripts
and basic texts in the symbolic interaction tradition were selected for
the listing; (4) authors of several theoretical chapters in the only
published symposium on symbolic interactionism were listed; and (5)
several authors of articles in the only book of general readings on
symbolic interactionism available in 1969 were also added to
the list. From this composite listing, and in consultation with three
well-known symbolic interactionists, Reynolds selected his final list of
124 potential respondents.
5 In the original list, certain words and phrases were underscored in each
definition.

Bibliographical index

Figures in square brackets indicate the pages in this book where the author concerned is cited.

AIKEN, H. D. (1962) 'Pragmatism and America's Philosophical Coming of Age,' pp. 47–81 in W. Barrett and H. D. Aiken (eds), *Philosophy in the Twentieth Century*, vol. 1, New York: Random House. [16]

BAKER, P. J. (1973) 'The Life Histories of W. I. Thomas and R. E. Park,' *American Journal of Sociology*, 79: 243–60. [124]

BALDWIN, J. M. (1895) *Mental Development in the Child and the Race*, New York: Macmillan. [12]

—— (1897) *Social and Ethical Interpretations in Mental Development*, New York: Macmillan. [12]

—— (1902) *Fragments in Philosophy and Science*, New York: Charles Scribner's Sons. [12]

BARNES, H. E. (1922) 'Some Contributions of American Psychological Sociology to Social and Political Theory,' *Sociological Review*, 13: 152–7. [27]

BARRETT, W. (1962) 'The Twentieth Century in its Philosophy,' pp. 19–43 in W. Barrett and H. D. Aiken (eds), *Philosophy in the Twentieth Century*, vol. 1, New York: Random House. [16]

BERGER, P. L. and T. LUCKMANN (1967) *The Social Construction of Reality*, New York: Doubleday. [53]

BITTNER, C. J. (1931) 'Mead's Social Concept of the Self,' *Sociology and Social Research*, 16: 6–22. [30, 40, 41]

BLOCK, F. (1973) 'Alternative Sociological Perspectives: Implications for Applied Sociology,' *Catalyst*, 7 (Winter): 29–41. [97]

BLUMER, H. (no date) 'Notes from G. H. Mead's Social Psychology Course.' [26]

—— (1937) 'Social Psychology,' pp. 144–98 in E. P. Schmidt (ed.), *Man and Society*, New York: Prentice-Hall. [4]

—— (1953) 'Psychological Import of the Human Group,' pp. 185–202 in M. Sherif and M. D. Wilson (eds), *Group Relations at the Crossroads*, New York: Harper & Brothers. [42, 63, 65]

—— (1954) 'What is Wrong with Social Theory?' American Sociological Review, 19: 3–10. [60]

—— (1962) 'Society as Symbolic Interaction,' pp. 179–92 in A. M. Rose (ed.), Human Behavior and Social Processes, Boston: Houghton Mifflin. [62, 120]

—— (1966) 'Sociological Implications of the Thought of G. H. Mead,' American Journal of Sociology, 71 (March): 535–44. [63]

—— (1969) Symbolic Interactionism, Englewood Cliffs: Prentice-Hall. [1, 2, 59, 118]

—— (1972) 'Action vs. Interaction,' review of Relations in Public, by E. Goffman, Society, 9 (April): 50–3. [72]

—— (1973) 'Comment on Symbolic Interaction as a Pragmatic Perspective: The Bias of Theory,' American Sociological Review, 38, no. 6 (December): 797–8. [126]

BODENHAFER, W. B. (1920–21) 'The Comparative Role of the Group Concept in Ward's Dynamic Sociology and Contemporary American Sociology,' American Journal of Sociology, 26: 425–74. [8]

BOGARDUS, E. S. (1940) The Development of Social Thought, New York: Longmans. [26]

BOOGS, S. T. (1956) 'An Interaction Study of Adult Socialization,' American Sociological Review, 21 (April): 191–8. [119]

BOSKOFF, A. (1969) Theory in American Sociology, New York: Thomas Y. Crowell. [22]

BRITTAN, A. (1973) Meanings and Situations, London: Routledge & Kegan Paul. [74, 83–5]

BROOKS, R. S. (1969) 'The Self and Political Role: A Symbolic Interactionist Approach to Political Ideology,' Sociological Quarterly, 10 (Winter): 22–31. [119]

BROTHERTON, B. W. (1943) 'The Genius of Pragmatic Empiricism: I,' Journal of Philosophy, 40: 14–21. [7]

BURKE, K. (1945) A Grammar of Motives, New York: Prentice-Hall. [68]

—— (1950) A Rhetoric of Motives, New York: Prentice-Hall. [68]

CHURCHILL, L. (1971) 'Ethnomethodology and Measurement,' Social Forces, 50 (December): 182–91. [78]

CICOUREL, A. V. (1964) Method and Measurement in Sociology, New York: Free Press. [79]

—— (1968) The Social Organization of Juvenile Justice, New York: Wiley. [78]

COLLINS, R. and M. MAKOWSKY (1972) The Discovery of Society, New York: Random House. [70, 72, 75, 79]

COOLEY, C. H. (1902) Human Nature and the Social Order, New York: Charles Scribner's Sons. [1, 10, 11, 12, 13]

—— (1909) *Social Organization*, New York: Charles Scribner's Sons.
[2, 9, 10, 12]

—— (1918) *Social Process*, New York: Charles Scribner's Sons. [9, 12, 15]

—— (1926) 'The Roots of Social Knowledge,' *American Journal of Sociology*, 32: 59–79. [10]

—— (1930) 'The Development of Sociology at Michigan,' pp. 3–19 in R. C. Angell (ed.), *Sociological Theory and Practice*, New York: Henry Holt. [8]

CORTI, W. R. (ed.) (1973) *The Philosophy of George Herbert Mead*, Winterthur, Switzerland: Archiv für genetische Philosophie. [28]

CRESSEY, D. R. (1969) *Theft of a Nation*, New York: Harper & Row. [120]

CURTIS, J. E. and J. W. PETRAS (eds) (1970) 'Introduction,' pp. 1–85 in *The Sociology of Knowledge: A. Reader*, New York: Praeger. [16]

CUZZORT, R. P. (1969) *Humanity and Modern Sociological Thought*, New York: Holt, Rinehart & Winston. [71]

DALTON, M. (1959) *Men Who Manage*, New York: Wiley. [120]

DAVIS, M. M. (1909) *Psychological Interpretations of Society*, New York: Longmans. [6]

DENZIN, N. K. (1969) 'Symbolic Interactionism and Ethnomethodology: A Proposed Synthesis,' *American Sociological Review*, 34 (December): 922–34. [86, 89–90]

—— (1970) 'Symbolic Interactionism and Ethnomethodology,' pp. 261–84 in J. D. Douglas (ed.), *Understanding Everyday Life*, Chicago: Aldine. [75]

—— (1972) 'The Genesis of Self in Early Childhood,' *Sociological Quarterly*, 13 (Summer): 291–314. [14]

DEUTSCHER, I. (1973) *What We Say/What We Do*, Glenview: Scott, Foresman & Company. [75, 82]

DEWEY, J. (1887) *Psychology*, New York: Harper & Brothers. [17]

—— (1896) 'The Reflex Arc Concept in Psychology,' *Psychological Review*, 3 (July): 357–70. [15, 18, 19, 44]

—— (1908) 'Does Reality Possess Practical Character?' pp. 53–80 in *Essays, Philosophical and Psychological, in Honor of W. James* (edited 'by his colleagues'), New York: Longmans. [15]

—— (1910) *The Influence of Darwin on Philosophy and Other Essays in Contemporary Thought*, New York: Henry Holt. [11]

—— (1915) *German Philosophy and Politics*, New York: G. P. Putnam & Sons. [16]

—— (1916) *Democracy and Education*, New York: Macmillan. [20]

—— (1917a) 'A Recovery of Philosophy,' pp. 3–69 in J. Dewey, A. W. Moore, H. C. Brown, G. H. Mead, B. H. Bode, H. W. Stuart, J. H.

Tufts, H. M. Kallen (eds), *Creative Intelligence*, New York: Henry Holt. [15, 16]
—— (1917b) 'The Need for Social Psychology,' *Psychological Review*, 24: 266–77. [19]
—— (1920) *Reconstruction in Philosophy*, New York: Henry Holt. [15, 21]
—— (1922) *Human Nature and Conduct*, New York: Henry Holt. [1, 17, 19]
—— (1925) *Experience and Nature*, New York: W. W. Norton. [5]
—— (1938) *Logic: The Theory of Inquiry*, New York: Henry Holt. [16]
DEXTER, L. A. (1962) 'On the Politics and Sociology of Stupidity in our Society,' *Social Problems*, 9 (Winter): 221–8. [110]
DOUGLAS, J. D. (ed.) (1970a) *The Impact of Sociology*, New York: Appleton-Century-Crofts. [79]
—— (ed.), (1970b) *The Relevance of Sociology*, New York: Appleton-Century-Crofts. [79]
—— (ed.), (1970c) *Understanding Everyday Life*, Chicago: Aldine; London: Routledge & Kegan Paul. [79]
DREITZEL, H. P. (ed.) (1970) *Recent Sociology*, no. 2, London: Macmillan. [53, 75, 79, 80]
DRIVER, E. D. (1969) 'Self-Conceptions in India and the United States: A Cross-cultural Validation of the Twenty Statement Test,' *Sociological Quarterly*, 10, no. 3 (Summer): 341–54. [119]
DUNCAN, H. D. (1968) *Symbols in Society*, New York: Oxford University Press. [2, 71]
EUBANK, E. E. (1926) 'The Concepts of Sociology,' *Social Forces* 5: 386–400. [52]
—— (1927) 'The Concept of the Group,' *Sociology and Social Research*, 12: 421–30. [42]
FARBERMAN, H. A. (1970) 'Mannheim, Cooley, and Mead: Toward a Social Theory of Mentality,' *Sociological Quarterly*, 11 (Winter): 3–13. [28]
FARIS, R. E. L. (1964) 'The Discipline of Sociology,' pp. 1–35 in *Handbook of Modern Sociology*, Chicago: Rand McNally. [51, 124]
—— (1967) *Chicago Sociology*, San Francisco: Chandler & Chandler. [124]
FILMER, P. (1972) 'On Harold Garfinkel's Ethnomethodology,' pp. 203–34 in P. Filmer *et al.*, *New Directions in Sociological Theory*, London: Collier-Macmillan. [75, 78]
FIRESTONE, S. (1971) *The Dialectic of Sex*, New York: Bantam Books. [19]
FISCH, M. H. (1950) 'Dewey's Place in the Classic Period of American Philosophy,' pp. 9–36 in K. D. Benne and W. D. Stanley (eds),

Essays for J. Dewey's Ninetieth Birthday, Urbana: Bureau of Research and Service, College of Education, University of Illinois. [16, 21]

FLETCHER, C. R. *et al.* (1974) 'The Labelling Theory of Mental Illness,' in P. Roman and H. Trice (eds), *Current Perspectives in Psychiatric Sociology*, Philadelphia: F. A. Davis. [108–9]

FREUD, S. (no date) *Civilization and its Discontents*, Garden City: Doubleday. [25]

GARFINKEL, H. (1967) *Studies in Ethnomethodology*, Englewood Cliffs: Prentice-Hall. [76, 77, 81]

GOFFMAN, E. (1959) *The Presentation of Self in Everyday Life*, Garden City: Doubleday. [68, 69, 85, 108]

—— (1961) *Asylums*, Garden City: Doubleday. [75]

—— (1963) *Stigma*, Englewood Cliffs: Prentice-Hall. [75]

—— (1967) *Interaction Ritual*, Garden City: Doubleday. [69, 93]

GOULDNER, A. W. (1961) 'Metaphysical Pathos and the Theory of Bureaucracy,' pp. 71–81 in Ametai Etzioni (ed.), *Complex Organizations: A Sociological Reader*, New York: Holt, Rinehart & Winston. [107]

—— (1970a) *The Coming Crisis in Western Sociology*, New York: Basic Books. [73, 74, 80, 98, 100, 106–11, 113]

—— (1970b) 'Review of N. J. Smelser and J. A. Davis' Sociology,' *American Sociological Review*, 35 (April): 332–4. [111–12]

GROSS, E. and G. P. STONE (1964) 'Embarrassment and the Analysis of Role Requirements,' *American Journal of Sociology*, 60 (July): 1–15. [93]

HALL, P. (1972) 'A Symbolic Interactionist Analysis of Politics,' *Sociological Inquiry*, 42, no. 3–4: 35–75. [86, 90–1, 119]

HAMILTON, W. H. (1931) 'Charles Horton Cooley,' pp. 355–6 in *Encyclopedia of the Social Sciences*, vol. 4, New York: Macmillan. [9]

HEAP, J. L. and P. A. ROTH (1973) 'On Phenomenological Sociology,' *American Sociological Review*, 38 (June): 354–67. [75]

HICKMAN, C. A. and M. H. KUHN (1956) *Individuals, Groups, and Economic Behavior*, New York: Dryden. [58, 64, 65, 89, 119]

HINKLE, G. J. (1972) ' "Forms" and "Types" in the Study of Human Behavior: An Examination of the Generalizing Concepts of Mead and Schutz,' *Kansas Journal of Sociology*, VIII (Fall): 91–110. [75]

HINKLE, R. C. (1963) 'Antecedents of the Action Orientation in American Sociology before 1935,' *American Sociological Review*, 28 (October): 705–15. [25]

—— (1967) 'Charles Horton Cooley's General Sociological Orientation,' *Sociological Quarterly*, 8 (Winter): 5–20. [9]

HOROWITZ, I. L. (1971) 'Review of Howard S. Becker's Sociological Work:

Method and Substance,' *American Sociological Review*, 36 (June):
527–8. [98, 103–4, 113]

HOUSE, F. (1936) *The Development of Sociology*, New York: McGraw-
Hill. [20]

HUBER, J. (1973a) 'Symbolic Interaction as a Pragmatic Perspective:
The Bias of Emergent Theory,' *American Sociological Review*, 38
(April): 278–84. [98, 100, 104–6, 124]

—— (1973b) 'Reply to Blumer: But Who Will Scrutinize the
Scrutinizers?' *American Sociological Review*, 38, no. 6 (December):
798–9. [126]

HUGHES, E. C. (1958) *Men and Their Work*, New York: Free Press.
[120]

HUMPHREYS, L. (1970) *Tearoom Trade*, Chicago: Aldine. [110]

JAMES, W. (1880) 'Great Men, Great Thoughts, and the Environment,'
Atlantic Monthly, 46: 441–59. [7]

—— (1890) *Principles of Psychology*, 2 vols, New York: Henry Holt.
[3, 4, 5, 6, 7, 18]

—— (1897) *The Will To Believe and Other Essays in Popular
Psychology*, New York: Longmans. [7]

—— (1907) *Pragmatism*, New York: Longmans. [7]

—— (1971) 'A Morality for Americans,' pp. 166–7 in G. Myers (ed.),
The Spirit of American Philosophy, New York: Capricorn. [123]

JANDY, E. C. (1942) *Charles Horton Cooley: His Life and His Social
Theory*, New York: Octagon. [8]

KANTER, R. M. (1972) 'Symbolic Interactionism and Politics in
Systematic Perspective,' *Sociological Inquiry*, 42, no. 3–4: 77–92. [97]

KONVITZ, M. R. and G. KENNEDY (eds) (1960) *The American Pragmatists*,
New York: Meridian. [123]

KUHN, M. H. (no date) 'Lectures on the Self,' mimeographed. [60, 64]

—— (1954) 'Factors in Personality: Socio-cultural Determinants as seen
through the Amish,' pp. 43–60 in F. L. K. Hsu (ed.), *Aspects of
Culture and Personality*, New York: Abelard-Schuman. [65, 89, 119]

—— (1964) 'Major Trends in Symbolic Interaction Theory in the Past
Twenty-five Years,' *Sociological Quarterly*, 5 (Winter): 61–84. [1, 54,
58, 86–9]

LANSTEIN, S. H. (1973) 'Mead (and Piaget) Notwithstanding: Symbolic
Interactionist Notes on the Pre-language Development of Self,'
unpublished paper presented at a meeting of the American Sociological
Association, New York, August. [14]

LASCH, C. (1965) *The New Radicalism in America 1889–1963*, New York:
Alfred Knopf. [97]

LEE, G. C. (1945) *George Herbert Mead, Philosopher of the Social
Individual*, New York: King's Crown. [34, 36, 39]

LEWIS, J. D. (1972) 'Peirce, Mead, and the Objectivity of Meaning,' *Kansas Journal of Sociology*, 8 (Fall): 111–22. [123]

LICHTMAN, R. T. (1970) 'Symbolic Interactionism and Social Reality: Some Marxist Queries,' *Berkeley Journal of Sociology*, 15:75–94. [100, 102–3]

LINCOURT, J. M. and P. H. HARE (1973) 'Neglected American Philosophers in the History of Symbolic Interactionism,' *Journal of the History of the Behavioral Sciences*, 9 (October): 333–8. [123]

LINDESMITH, A. and A. STRAUSS (1968) *Social Psychology*, New York: Holt, Rinehart & Winston. [2]

LOFLAND, J. (1970) 'Interactionist Imagery and Analytic Interruptus,' pp. 35–45 in T. Shibutani (ed.), *Human Nature and Collective Behavior*, Englewood Cliffs: Prentice-Hall. [68]

LYMAN, S. M. and M. B. SCOTT (1970) *A Sociology of the Absurd*, New York: Appleton-Century-Crofts. [71]

MACANDREW, C. and R. EDGERTON (1969) *Drunken Comportment: A Social Explanation*, Chicago: Aldine. [78]

MCHUGH, P. (1968) *Defining the Situation*, Indianapolis: Bobbs-Merrill. [78]

MALINOWSKI, B. (1944) *A Scientific Theory of Culture*, Chapel Hill: North Carolina University Press. [101]

MANIS, J. G. (1972) 'Common Sense and Analytic Sociology,' *Sociological Focus*, 5 (Spring): 1–15. [101]

MANIS, J. G. and B. N. MELTZER (eds) (1967) *Symbolic Interaction*, Boston: Allyn & Bacon. [53]

—— (1972) *Symbolic Interaction* (second edition), Boston: Allyn & Bacon. [2, 53, 121]

MARTINDALE, D. (1960) *American Society*, Princeton: Van Nostrand. [73]

MAYRL, W. W. (1973) 'Ethnomethodology: Sociology without Society,' *Catalyst*, 7 (Winter): 15–28. [98–9]

MEAD, G. H. (1896) 'The Relations of Play to Education,' *University of Chicago Record*, 1: 140–5. [29]

—— (1899) 'The Working Hypothesis in Social Reform,' *American Journal of Sociology*, 5: 367–71. [14, 31]

—— (1900) 'Suggestions Toward a Theory of the Philosophical Disciplines,' *Philosophical Review*, 9: 1–17. [32]

—— (1903) 'The Basis for a Parent's Association,' *Elementary School Teacher*, 8: 337–46. [29]

—— (1904) 'The Relation of Psychology and Philosophy,' *Psychological Bulletin*, 1: 375–91. [36]

—— (1905) 'Review of D. Draghicesco's *Du Rôle de l'individu dans le déterminisme social*,' *Psychological Bulletin*, 2: 399–405. [31]

—— (1906) 'The Imagination in Wundt's Treatment of Myth and Religion,' *Psychological Bulletin*, 3 : 393–9. [32]

—— (1907a) 'Concerning Animal Perception,' *Psychological Review*, 14 : 383–9. [32]

—— (1907b) 'Policy of the Elementary School Teacher,' *Elementary School Teacher*, 8 : 281–4. [30]

—— (1907c) 'The Relation of Imitation to the Theory of Animal Perception,' *Psychological Bulletin*, 5 : 210–11. [32]

—— (1908) 'Industrial Education and the Working Man and the School,' *Elementary School Teacher*, 9 : 369–83. [30]

—— (1910a) 'Psychology of Social Consciousness Implied in Instruction,' *Science*, 31 : 688–93. [30]

—— (1910b) 'What Social Objects must Psychology Presuppose?' *Journal of Philosophy*, 7 : 174–80. [34, 40]

—— (1912a) 'Exhibit of the City Club Committee on Public Education,' *City Club Bulletin*, 5 : 9. [30]

—— (1912b) 'The Mechanism of Social Consciousness,' *Journal of Philosophy*, 9 : 401–6. [31, 35, 41]

—— (1917) 'The Psychology of Punitive Justice,' *American Journal of Sociology*, 23 : 577–602. [35, 41]

—— (1922) 'A Behavioristic Account of the Significant Symbol,' *Journal of Philosophy*, 19 : 157–63. [30]

—— (1923) 'Scientific Method and the Moral Sciences,' *International Journal of Ethics*, 33 : 224–47. [39]

—— (1924) 'The Genesis of the Self and Social Control,' *International Journal of Ethics*, 35 : 251–77. [37]

—— (1930) 'The Philosophies of Royce, James, and Dewey in their American Setting,' pp. 75–105 in W. H. Kirkpatrick and H. R. Linwell (eds), *John Dewey: The Man and His Philosophy*, Cambridge : Harvard University. [36]

—— (1932) *The Philosophy of the Present*, edited by A. E. Murphy with prefatory remarks by J. Dewey, Chicago : Open Court. [2, 36, 38, 39, 40, 41]

—— (1934) *Mind, Self and Society*, edited with introduction by C. W. Morris, University of Chicago. [1, 8, 28, 31, 36, 40, 49]

—— (1936) *Movements of Thought in the Nineteenth Century*, edited by M. H. Moore, University of Chicago. [11, 80]

—— (1938) *The Philosophy of the Act*, edited with introduction by C. W. Morris in collaboration with J. M. Brewster, A. M. Dunham and D. L. Miller, University of Chicago. [33, 35, 36]

MELTZER, B. N. (1959) *The Social Psychology of George Herbert Mead*, Kalamazoo : Center for Sociological Research, Western Michigan University. [82–5]

—— (1972) 'Mead's Social Psychology,' pp. 4–22 in J. G. Manis and B. N. Meltzer (eds), *Symbolic Interaction: A Reader in Social Psychology*, Boston: Allyn & Bacon. [83–5, 93]

MELTZER, B. N. and J. W. PETRAS (1970) 'The Chicago and Iowa Schools of Symbolic Interactionism,' pp. 3–17 in T. Shibutani (ed.), *Human Nature and Collective Behavior*, Englewood Cliffs: Prentice-Hall. [1, 53, 123, 124, 125]

MERRILL, F. E. (1961) 'Stendhal and the Self: A Study in the Sociology of Literature,' *American Journal of Sociology*, 66 (March): 446–53. [119]

MESSINGER, S. E. with H. SAMPSON and R. D. TOWNE (1962) 'Life as Theater: Some Notes on the Dramaturgic Approach to Social Reality,' *Sociometry*, 25 (September): 98–110. [72]

MILLER, D. L. (1972) 'The Meaning of Sameness or Family Resemblance in the Pragmatic Tradition,' *Tulane Studies in Philosophy*, 21: 51–62. [28]

—— (1973a) *George Herbert Mead: Self, Language, and the World*, Austin and London: University of Texas Press. [28]

—— (1973b) 'George Herbert Mead: Symbolic Interaction and Social Change,' *Psychological Record*, 23: 294–304. [28]

MILLS, C. W. (1966) *Sociology and Pragmatism*, New York: Oxford University Press. [123]

MULLINS, N. C. with the assistance of C. J. MULLINS (1973) *Theories and Theory Groups in Contemporary American Sociology*, New York: Harper & Row. [79, 96, 100, 125]

MURPHY, A. E. (1932) 'Introduction,' pp. xi–xxxv in G. H. Mead (1932), *Philosophy of the Present*, Chicago: Open Court. [39]

NATANSON, M. (1956) *The Social Dynamics of George H. Mead*, Washington, D.C.: Public Affairs Press. [97]

NICOLAUS, M. (1970) 'Remarks at the ASA Convention,' pp. 274–8 in L. T. Reynolds and J. M. Reynolds (eds), *The Sociology of Sociology*, New York: McKay. [112]

OGBURN, W. F. (1922) *Social Change*, New York: Huebsch. [25]

O'KELLY, C. and J. W. PETRAS (1970) 'Images of Man in Early American Sociology, Part II: The Changing Concept of Social Reform,' *Journal of the History of the Behavioral Sciences*, 6 (October): 317–34. [5]

OVERINGTON, M. A. (1971) 'The Image of Man in Symbolic Interactionism'

PARK, R. and E. BURGESS (1921) *Introduction to the Science of Sociology*, unpublished Master's thesis, University of Wisconsin. [1, 7] University of Chicago. [51]

PARSONS, T. (1964) 'Recent Trends in Structural-functional Theory,' in

Methodological Stances in Symbolic Interactionism,' *Sociological Quarterly*, 14 (Spring): 189–99. [53, 57]

REYNOLDS, J. M. and L. T. REYNOLDS (1973) 'Interactionism, Complicity and the Astructural Bias,' *Catalyst*, 7 (Winter): 76–85. [113, 125]

RIEZLER, K. (1943) 'Comment on the Social Psychology of Shame,' *American Journal of Sociology*, 48 (January): 457–65. [93]

ROPERS, R. (1973) 'Mead, Marx and Social Psychology,' *Catalyst*, 7 (Winter): 42–61. [97]

ROSE, A. M. (ed.) (1962) *Human Behavior and Social Processes*, Boston: Houghton-Mifflin; London: Routledge & Kegan Paul. [2]

—— (1967) *The Power Structure*, New York: Oxford University Press. [91, 119]

RQSE, A. M. and C. B. ROSE (1969) *Sociology: The Study of Human Relations*, New York: Alfred Knopf. [85]

ROSS, E. A. (1908) *Social Psychology*, New York: Macmillan. [123]

SCHWENDINGER, J. and H. SCHWENDINGER (1971) 'Sociology's Founding Factors: Sexists to the Man,' *Journal of Marriage and the Family*, 33 (November): 783–99. [42]

SHASKOLSKY, L. (1970) 'The Development of Sociological Theory in America—a Sociology of Knowledge Interpretation,' pp. 6–30 in L. T. and J. M. Reynolds (eds), *The Sociology of Sociology*, New York: McKay. [56, 98, 100–2, 113]

SHIBUTANI, T. (1961) *Society and Personality*, Englewood Cliffs: Prentice-Hall. [2, 26, 33, 93]

SHIBUTANI, T. and K. M. KWAN (1965) *Ethnic Stratification*, New York: Macmillan. [120]

SJOBERG, G. and R. NETT (1968) *A Methodology for Social Research*, New York: Harper & Row. [60]

SMITH, D. L. (1973a) 'Symbolic Interactionism: Definitions of the Situation from H. Becker and J. Lofland,' *Catalyst*, 7 (Winter): 62–75. [97]

—— (1973b) 'Science: The Knowledge Producing Appendage,' pp. 145–70 in L. T. Reynolds and J. M. Henslin (eds), *American Society: A Critical Analysis*, New York: McKay. [112]

SPITZER, S., C. COUCH and J. STRATTON (no date) *The Assessment of Self*, Iowa City: Escort-Sernoll. [60]

STRAUSS, A. (1963) 'The Hospital and its Negotiated Order,' pp. 147-70 in E. Freidson (ed.), *The Hospital in Modern Society*, New York: Free Press. [109, 125]

—— (ed.) (1964) *George Herbert Mead on Social Psychology*, Chicago: Phoenix. [125]

SUDNOW, D. (1967) *Passing On: The Social Organization of Dying*, Englewood Cliffs: Prentice-Hall. [78]

SWANSON, G. (1968) 'Symbolic Interaction,' pp. 441–5 in D. Sills (ed.), *International Encyclopedia of the Social Sciences*, vol. 4, New York: Macmillan. [1]

THOMAS, W. I. (1896) 'The Scope and Method of Folk Psychology,' *American Journal of Sociology*, 1: 434–45. [22, 24]

—— (1900) 'The Gaming Instinct,' *American Journal of Sociology*, 6: 750–63. [124]

—— (1906) 'The Adventitious Character of Women,' *American Journal of Sociology*, 13: 32–44. [25]

—— (1907) *Sex and Society*, University of Chicago. [22, 24]

—— (1909) *Source Book for Social Origins*, University of Chicago. [26]

—— (1923) *The Unadjusted Girl*, Boston: Little, Brown. [1, 22, 25]

THOMAS, W. I. and F. ZNANIECKI (1918) *The Polish Peasant in Europe and America*, 5 vols, Boston: Richard Badger. [22, 27, 51]

TONNESS, A. (1932) 'A Notation on the Problems of the Past—with Empirical Reference to George Herbert Mead,' *Journal of Philosophy*, 29: 599–606. [38]

TREMMEL, W. C. (1957) 'The Social Concepts of George Herbert Mead,' pp. 1–36 in the *Emporia State Research Studies*, 5, para. 4. [28, 37, 49]

TROYER, J. L. (1946) 'Mead's Social and Functional Theory of Mind,' *American Sociological Review*, 11: 198–202. [35]

TUCKER, C. W. (1966) 'Some Methodological Problems of Kuhn's Self Theory,' *Sociological Quarterly*, 7 (Summer): 345–58. [59, 125]

TUCKER, C. W. and J. STOECKEL (1969) 'The Epistemological Assumptions of Symbolic Interactionism and Social Behaviorism,' unpublished paper presented at a meeting of the American Sociological Association, San Francisco, August. [1, 124]

TURNER, R. H. (1962) 'Role-Taking: Process versus Conformity,' pp. 20–40 in A. M. Rose (ed.), *Human Behavior and Social Processes*, Boston: Houghton-Mifflin. [64]

TURNER, R. and L. KILLIAN (1957) *Collective Behavior*, Englewood Cliffs: Prentice-Hall. [120]

VAUGHAN, T. R. and L. T. REYNOLDS (1968) 'The Sociology of Symbolic Interactionism,' *American Sociologist*, 3 (August): 208–14. [1, 53, 57, 113]

VEBLEN, T. (1899) *The Theory of the Leisure Class*, New York: Macmillan. [123]

VOLKART, E. H. (ed.) (1951) *Social Behavior and Personality*, New York: Social Science Research Council. [25, 27]

WALLACE, W. L. (ed.) (1969) *Sociological Theory*, Chicago: Aldine. [75]

WARSHAY, L. (1971) 'The Current State of Sociological Theory: Diversity, Polarity, Empiricism, and Small Theories,' *Sociological Quarterly*, 12 (Winter): 23–45. [54, 75, 80]

WELLS, H. K. (1971) *Pragmatism: Philosophy of Imperialism*, New York : Books for Libraries Press. [97]

WHITE, M. (1963) *Social Thoughts in America*, Boston : Beacon Press. [16]

WILLIAMS, W. A. (1966) *The Contours of American History*, Chicago : Quadrangle. [97]

WINSTON, E. and W. F. OGBURN (1929) 'The Frequency and Probability of Insanity,' *American Journal of Sociology* 34 : 822–31. [25]

WRONG, D. H. (1961) 'The Over-Socialized Conception of Man,' *American Sociological Review*, 26 (April) : 185–93. [64]

ZIMMERMAN, D. H. and D. L. WIEDER (1970) 'Ethnomethodology and the Problem of Order : Comments on Denzin,' pp. 287–95 in J. D. Douglas (ed.), *Understanding Everyday Life*, Chicago : Aldine. [75]

Index

Routledge Social Science Series

Routledge & Kegan Paul   London, Henley and Boston

39 Store Street,
London WC1E 7DD
Broadway House,
Newtown Road,
Henley-on-Thames,
Oxon RG9 1EN
9 Park Street,
Boston, Mass. 02108

Contents

*Authors wishing to submit manuscripts for any series
in this catalogue should send them to the Social Science Editor,
Routledge & Kegan Paul Ltd, 39 Store Street,
London WC1E 7DD.*
● *Books so marked are available in paperback.*
○ *Books so marked are available in paperback only.*
*All books are in metric Demy 8vo format (216 × 138mm approx.)
unless otherwise stated.*

International Library of Sociology
General Editor John Rex

GENERAL SOCIOLOGY

Barnsley, J. H. The Social Reality of Ethics. *464 pp.*
Brown, Robert. Explanation in Social Science. *208 pp.*
● Rules and Laws in Sociology. *192 pp.*
Bruford, W. H. Chekhov and His Russia. *A Sociological Study. 244 pp.*
Burton, F. and **Carlen, P.** Official Discourse. *On Discourse Analysis, Government Publications, Ideology. About 140 pp.*
Cain, Maureen E. Society and the Policeman's Role. *326 pp.*
● **Fletcher, Colin.** Beneath the Surface. *An Account of Three Styles of Sociological Research. 221 pp.*
Gibson, Quentin. The Logic of Social Enquiry. *240 pp.*
Glassner, B. Essential Interactionism. *208 pp.*
Glucksmann, M. Structuralist Analysis in Contemporary Social Thought. *212 pp.*
Gurvitch, Georges. Sociology of Law. *Foreword by Roscoe Pound. 264 pp.*
Hinkle, R. Founding Theory of American Sociology 1881–1913. *About 350 pp.*
Homans, George C. Sentiments and Activities. *336 pp.*
Johnson, Harry M. Sociology: *A Systematic Introduction. Foreword by Robert K. Merton. 710 pp.*
● **Keat, Russell** and **Urry, John.** Social Theory as Science. *278 pp.*
Mannheim, Karl. Essays on Sociology and Social Psychology. *Edited by Paul Keckskemeti. With Editorial Note by Adolph Lowe. 344 pp.*
Martindale, Don. The Nature and Types of Sociological Theory. *292 pp.*
● **Maus, Heinz.** A Short History of Sociology. *234 pp.*
Myrdal, Gunnar. Value in Social Theory: *A Collection of Essays on Methodology. Edited by Paul Streeten. 332 pp.*
Ogburn, William F. and **Nimkoff, Meyer F.** A Handbook of Sociology. *Preface by Karl Mannheim. 656 pp. 46 figures. 35 tables.*
Parsons, Talcott and **Smelser, Neil J.** Economy and Society: *A Study in the Integration of Economic and Social Theory. 362 pp.*
Payne, G., Dingwall, R., Payne, J. and **Carter, M.** Sociology and Social Research. *About 250 pp.*
Podgórecki, A. Practical Social Sciences. *About 200 pp.*
Podgórecki, A. and **Łos, M.** Multidimensional Sociology. *268 pp.*
Raffel, S. Matters of Fact. *A Sociological Inquiry. 152 pp.*
● **Rex, John.** Key Problems of Sociological Theory. *220 pp.*
Sociology and the Demystification of the Modern World. *282 pp.*
● **Rex, John.** (Ed.) Approaches to Sociology. *Contributions by Peter Abell, Frank Bechhofer, Basil Bernstein, Ronald Fletcher, David Frisby, Miriam Glucksmann, Peter Lassman, Herminio Martins, John Rex, Roland Robertson, John Westergaard and Jock Young. 302 pp.*
Rigby, A. Alternative Realities. *352 pp.*
Roche, M. Phenomenology, Language and the Social Sciences. *374 pp.*
Sahay, A. Sociological Analysis. *220 pp.*
Strasser, Hermann. The Normative Structure of Sociology. *Conservative and Emancipatory Themes in Social Thought. About 340 pp.*
Strong, P. Ceremonial Order of the Clinic. *267 pp.*
Urry, John. Reference Groups and the Theory of Revolution. *244 pp.*
Weinberg, E. Development of Sociology in the Soviet Union. *173 pp.*

FOREIGN CLASSICS OF SOCIOLOGY

● **Gerth, H. H.** and **Mills, C. Wright.** From Max Weber: *Essays in Sociology. 502 pp.*

● **Tönnies, Ferdinand.** Community and Association *(Gemeinschaft und Gesell-schaft).\Translated and Supplemented by Charles P. Loomis. Foreword by Pitirim A. Sorokin. 334 pp.*

SOCIAL STRUCTURE

Andreski, Stanislav. Military Organization and Society. *Foreword by Professor A. R. Radcliffe-Brown. 226 pp. 1 folder.*

Broom, L., Lancaster Jones, F., McDonnell, P. and **Williams, T.** The Inheritance of Inequality. *About 180 pp.*

Carlton, Eric. Ideology and Social Order. *Foreword by Professor Philip Abrahams. About 320 pp.*

Clegg, S. and **Dunkerley, D.** Organization, Class and Control. *614 pp.*

Coontz, Sydney H. Population Theories and the Economic Interpretation. *202 pp.*

Coser, Lewis. The Functions of Social Conflict. *204 pp.*

Crook, I. and **D.** The First Years of the Yangyi Commune. *304 pp., illustrated.*

Dickie-Clark, H. F. Marginal Situation: *A Sociological Study of a Coloured Group. 240 pp. 11 tables.*

Giner, S. and **Archer, M. S.** (Eds) Contemporary Europe: *Social Structures and Cultural Patterns, 336 pp.*

● **Glaser, Barney** and **Strauss, Anselm L.** Status Passage: *A Formal Theory. 212 pp.*

Glass, D. V. (Ed.) Social Mobility in Britain. *Contributions by J. Berent, T. Bottomore, R. C. Chambers, J. Floud, D. V. Glass, J. R. Hall, H. T. Himmelweit, R. K. Kelsall, F. M. Martin, C. A. Moser, R. Mukherjee and W. Ziegel. 420 pp.*

Kelsall, R. K. Higher Civil Servants in Britain: *From 1870 to the Present Day. 268 pp. 31 tables.*

● **Lawton, Denis.** Social Class, Language and Education. *192 pp.*

McLeish, John. The Theory of Social Change: *Four Views Considered. 128 pp.*

● **Marsh, David C.** The Changing Social Structure of England and Wales, 1871–1961. *Revised edition. 288 pp.*

Menzies, Ken. Talcott Parsons and the Social Image of Man. *About 208 pp.*

● **Mouzelis, Nicos.** Organization and Bureaucracy. *An Analysis of Modern Theories. 240 pp.*

● **Ossowski, Stanislaw.** Class Structure in the Social Consciousness. *210 pp.*

● **Podgórecki, Adam.** Law and Society. *302 pp.*

Renner, Karl. Institutions of Private Law and Their Social Functions. *Edited, with an Introduction and Notes, by O. Kahn-Freud. Translated by Agnes Schwarzschild. 316 pp.*

Rex, J. and **Tomlinson, S.** Colonial Immigrants in a British City. *A Class Analysis. 368 pp.*

Smooha, S. Israel: Pluralism and Conflict. *472 pp.*

Wesolowski, W. Class, Strata and Power. *Trans. and with Introduction by G. Kolankiewicz. 160 pp.*

Zureik, E. Palestinians in Israel. *A Study in Internal Colonialism. 264 pp.*

SOCIOLOGY AND POLITICS

Acton, T. A. Gypsy Politics and Social Change. *316 pp.*

Burton, F. Politics of Legitimacy. *Struggles in a Belfast Community. 250 pp.*

Crook, I. and **D.** Revolution in a Chinese Village. *Ten Mile Inn. 216 pp., illustrated.*

Etzioni-Halevy, E. Political Manipulation and Administrative Power. *A Comparative Study. About 200 pp.*

Fielding, N. The National Front. *About 250 pp.*

● **Hechter, Michael.** Internal Colonialism. *The Celtic Fringe in British National Development, 1536–1966. 380 pp.*

Kornhauser, William. The Politics of Mass Society. *272 pp. 20 tables.*

Korpi, W. The Working Class in Welfare Capitalism. *Work, Unions and Politics in Sweden. 472 pp.*

Kroes, R. Soldiers and Students. *A Study of Right- and Left-wing Students. 174 pp.*

Martin, Roderick. Sociology of Power. *About 272 pp.*

Merquior, J. G. Rousseau and Weber. *A Study in the Theory of Legitimacy. About 288 pp.*

Myrdal, Gunnar. The Political Element in the Development of Economic Theory. *Translated from the German by Paul Streeten. 282 pp.*

Varma, B. N. The Sociology and Politics of Development. *A Theoretical Study. 236 pp.*

Wong, S.-L. Sociology and Socialism in Contemporary China. *160 pp.*

Wootton, Graham. Workers, Unions and the State. *188 pp.*

CRIMINOLOGY

Ancel, Marc. Social Defence: *A Modern Approach to Criminal Problems. Foreword by Leon Radzinowicz. 240 pp.*

Athens, L. Violent Criminal Acts and Actors. *104 pp.*

Cain, Maureen E. Society and the Policeman's Role. *326 pp.*

Cloward, Richard A. and **Ohlin, Lloyd E.** Delinquency and Opportunity: *A Theory of Delinquent Gangs. 248 pp.*

Downes, David M. The Delinquent Solution. *A Study in Subcultural Theory. 296 pp.*

Friedlander, Kate. The Psycho-Analytical Approach to Juvenile Delinquency: *Theory, Case Studies, Treatment. 320 pp.*

Gleuck, Sheldon and **Eleanor.** Family Environment and Delinquency. *With the statistical assistance of Rose W. Kneznek. 340 pp.*

Lopez-Rey, Manuel. Crime. *An Analytical Appraisal. 288 pp.*

Mannheim, Hermann. Comparative Criminology: *A Text Book. Two volumes. 442 pp. and 380 pp.*

Morris, Terence. The Criminal Area: *A Study in Social Ecology. Foreword by Hermann Mannheim. 232 pp. 25 tables. 4 maps.*

Rock, Paul. Making People Pay. *338 pp.*

● **Taylor, Ian, Walton, Paul** and **Young, Jock.** The New Criminology. *For a Social Theory of Deviance. 325 pp.*

● **Taylor, Ian, Walton, Paul** and **Young, Jock.** (Eds) Critical Criminology. *268 pp.*

SOCIAL PSYCHOLOGY

Bagley, Christopher. The Social Psychology of the Epileptic Child. *320 pp.*

Brittan, Arthur. Meanings and Situations. *224 pp.*

Carroll, J. Break-Out from the Crystal Palace. *200 pp.*

● **Fleming, C. M.** Adolescence: Its Social Psychology. *With an Introduction to recent findings from the fields of Anthropology, Physiology, Medicine, Psychometrics and Sociometry. 288 pp.*

● The Social Psychology of Education: *An Introduction and Guide to Its Study. 136 pp.*

Linton, Ralph. The Cultural Background of Personality. *132 pp.*

● **Mayo, Elton.** The Social Problems of an Industrial Civilization. *With an Appendix on the Political Problem. 180 pp.*

Ottaway, A. K. C. Learning Through Group Experience. *176 pp.*

Plummer, Ken. Sexual Stigma. *An Interactionist Account. 254 pp.*

● **Rose, Arnold M.** (Ed.) Human Behaviour and Social Processes: *an Interactionist Approach. Contributions by Arnold M. Rose, Ralph H. Turner, Anselm Strauss, Everett C. Hughes, E. Franklin Frazier, Howard S. Becker et al. 696 pp.*

Smelser, Neil J. Theory of Collective Behaviour. *448 pp.*

Stephenson, Geoffrey M. The Development of Conscience. *128 pp.*

Young, Kimball. Handbook of Social Psychology. *658 pp. 16 figures. 10 tables.*

SOCIOLOGY OF THE FAMILY

Bell, Colin R. Middle Class Families: *Social and Geographical Mobility. 224 pp.*
Burton, Lindy. Vulnerable Children. *272 pp.*
Gavron, Hannah. The Captive Wife: *Conflicts of Household Mothers. 190 pp.*
George, Victor and **Wilding, Paul.** Motherless Families. *248 pp.*
Klein, Josephine. Samples from English Cultures.
   1. Three Preliminary Studies and Aspects of Adult Life in England. *447 pp.*
   2. Child-Rearing Practices and Index. *247 pp.*
Klein, Viola. The Feminine Character. *History of an Ideology. 244 pp.*
McWhinnie, Alexina M. Adopted Children. *How They Grow Up. 304 pp.*
● **Morgan, D. H. J.** Social Theory and the Family. *About 320 pp.*
● **Myrdal, Alva** and **Klein, Viola.** Women's Two Roles: *Home and Work. 238 pp.*
   27 tables.
Parsons, Talcott and **Bales, Robert F.** Family: Socialization and Interaction Process.
   In collaboration with James Olds, Morris Zelditch and Philip E. Slater. 456 pp.
   50 figures and tables.

SOCIAL SERVICES

Bastide, Roger. The Sociology of Mental Disorder. *Translated from the French by
   Jean McNeil. 260 pp.*
Carlebach, Julius. Caring For Children in Trouble. *266 pp.*
George, Victor. Foster Care. *Theory and Practice. 234 pp.*
   Social Security: *Beveridge and After. 258 pp.*
George, V. and **Wilding, P.** Motherless Families. *248 pp.*
● **Goetschius, George W.** Working with Community Groups. *256 pp.*
Goetschius, George W. and **Tash, Joan.** Working with Unattached Youth. *416 pp.*
Heywood, Jean S. Children in Care. *The Development of the Service for the Deprived
   Child. Third revised edition. 284 pp.*
King, Roy D., Ranes, Norma V. and **Tizard, Jack.** Patterns of Residential Care.
   356 pp.
Leigh, John. Young People and Leisure. *256 pp.*
● **Mays, John.** (Ed.) Penelope Hall's Social Services of England and Wales.
   368 pp.
Morris, Mary. Voluntary Work and the Welfare State. *300 pp.*
Nokes, P. L. The Professional Task in Welfare Practice. *152 pp.*
Timms, Noel. Psychiatric Social Work in Great Britain (1939–1962). *280 pp.*
●   Social Casework: *Principles and Practice. 256 pp.*

SOCIOLOGY OF EDUCATION

Banks, Olive. Parity and Prestige in English Secondary Education: a Study in
   Educational Sociology. *272 pp.*
● **Blyth, W. A. L.** English Primary Education. *A Sociological Description.*
   2. Background. *168 pp.*
Collier, K. G. The Social Purposes of Education: *Personal and Social Values in
   Education. 268 pp.*
Evans, K. M. Sociometry and Education. *158 pp.*
● **Ford, Julienne.** Social Class and the Comprehensive School. *192 pp.*
Foster, P. J. Education and Social Change in Ghana. *336 pp. 3 maps.*
Fraser, W. R. Education and Society in Modern France. *150 pp.*
Grace, Gerald R. Role Conflict and the Teacher. *150 pp.*
Hans, Nicholas. New Trends in Education in the Eighteenth Century. *278 pp.*
   19 tables.
●   Comparative Education: *A Study of Educational Factors and Traditions. 360 pp.*
● **Hargreaves, David.** Interpersonal Relations and Education. *432 pp.*
●   Social Relations in a Secondary School. *240 pp.*
   School Organization and Pupil Involvement. *A Study of Secondary Schools.*

● **Mannheim, Karl** and **Stewart, W. A. C.** An Introduction to the Sociology of Education. *206 pp.*

● **Musgrove, F.** Youth and the Social Order. *176 pp.*

● **Ottaway, A. K. C.** Education and Society: An Introduction to the Sociology of Education. *With an Introduction by W. O. Lester Smith. 212 pp.*

Peers, Robert. Adult Education: *A Comparative Study. Revised edition. 398 pp.*

Stratta, Erica. The Education of Borstal Boys. *A Study of their Educational Experiences prior to, and during, Borstal Training. 256 pp.*

● **Taylor, P. H., Reid, W. A.** and **Holley, B. J.** The English Sixth Form. *A Case Study in Curriculum Research. 198 pp.*

SOCIOLOGY OF CULTURE

Eppel, E. M. and **M.** Adolescents and Morality: *A Study of some Moral Values and Dilemmas of Working Adolescents in the Context of a changing Climate of Opinion. Foreword by W. J. H. Sprott. 268 pp. 39 tables.*

● **Fromm, Erich.** The Fear of Freedom. *286 pp.*

● The Sane Society. *400 pp.*

Johnson, L. The Cultural Critics. *From Matthew Arnold to Raymond Williams. 233 pp.*

Mannheim, Karl. Essays on the Sociology of Culture. *Edited by Ernst Mannheim in co-operation with Paul Kecskemeti. Editorial Note by Adolph Lowe. 280 pp.*

Merquior, J. G. The Veil and the Mask. *Essays on Culture and Ideology. Foreword by Ernest Gellner. 140 pp.*

Zijderfeld, A. C. On Clichés. *The Supersedure of Meaning by Function in Modernity. 150 pp.*

SOCIOLOGY OF RELIGION

Argyle, Michael and **Beit-Hallahmi, Benjamin.** The Social Psychology of Religion. *256 pp.*

Glasner, Peter E. The Sociology of Secularisation. *A Critique of a Concept. 146 pp.*

Hall, J. R. The Ways Out. *Utopian Communal Groups in an Age of Babylon. 280 pp.*

Ranson, S., Hinings, B. and **Bryman, A.** Clergy, Ministers and Priests. *216 pp.*

Stark, Werner. The Sociology of Religion. *A Study of Christendom.*

Volume II. *Sectarian Religion. 368 pp.*

Volume III. *The Universal Church. 464 pp.*

Volume IV. *Types of Religious Man. 352 pp.*

Volume V. *Types of Religious Culture. 464 pp.*

Turner, B. S. Weber and Islam. *216 pp.*

Watt, W. Montgomery. Islam and the Integration of Society. *320 pp.*

SOCIOLOGY OF ART AND LITERATURE

Jarvie, Ian C. Towards a Sociology of the Cinema. *A Comparative Essay on the Structure and Functioning of a Major Entertainment Industry. 405 pp.*

Rust, Frances S. Dance in Society. *An Analysis of the Relationships between the Social Dance and Society in England from the Middle Ages to the Present Day. 256 pp. 8 pp. of plates.*

Schücking, L. L. The Sociology of Literary Taste. *112 pp.*

Wolff, Janet. Hermeneutic Philosophy and the Sociology of Art. *150 pp.*

SOCIOLOGY OF KNOWLEDGE

Diesing, P. Patterns of Discovery in the Social Sciences. *262 pp.*

● **Douglas, J. D.** (Ed.) Understanding Everyday Life. *370 pp.*

● **Hamilton, P.** Knowledge and Social Structure. *174 pp.*

Jarvie, I. C. Concepts and Society. *232 pp.*

Mannheim, Karl. Essays on the Sociology of Knowledge. *Edited by Paul Kecskemeti. Editorial Note by Adolph Lowe. 353 pp.*

Remmling, Gunter W. The Sociology of Karl Mannheim. *With a Bibliographical Guide to the Sociology of Knowledge, Ideological Analysis, and Social Planning. 255 pp.*

Remmling, Gunter W. (Ed.) Towards the Sociology of Knowledge. *Origin and Development of a Sociological Thought Style. 463 pp.*

Scheler, M. Problems of a Sociology of Knowledge. *Trans. by M. S. Frings. Edited and with an Introduction by K. Stikkers. 232 pp.*

URBAN SOCIOLOGY

Aldridge, M. The British New Towns. *A Programme Without a Policy. 232 pp.*

Ashworth, William. The Genesis of Modern British Town Planning: *A Study in Economic and Social History of the Nineteenth and Twentieth Centuries. 288 pp.*

Brittan, A. The Privatised World. *196 pp.*

Cullingworth, J. B. Housing Needs and Planning Policy: *A Restatement of the Problems of Housing Need and 'Overspill' in England and Wales. 232 pp. 44 tables. 8 maps.*

Dickinson, Robert E. City and Region: *A Geographical Interpretation. 608 pp. 125 figures.*

The West European City: *A Geographical Interpretation. 600 pp. 129 maps. 29 plates.*

Humphreys, Alexander J. New Dubliners: *Urbanization and the Irish Family. Foreword by George C. Homans. 304 pp.*

Jackson, Brian. Working Class Community: *Some General Notions raised by a Series of Studies in Northern England. 192 pp.*

● **Mann, P. H.** An Approach to Urban Sociology. *240 pp.*

Mellor, J. R. Urban Sociology in an Urbanized Society. *326 pp.*

Morris, R. N. and **Mogey, J.** The Sociology of Housing. *Studies at Berinsfield. 232 pp. 4 pp. plates.*

Mullan, R. Stevenage Ltd. *About 250 pp.*

Rex, J. and **Tomlinson, S.** Colonial Immigrants in a British City. *A Class Analysis. 368 pp.*

Rosser, C. and **Harris, C.** The Family and Social Change. *A Study of Family and Kinship in a South Wales Town. 352 pp. 8 maps.*

● **Stacey, Margaret, Batsone, Eric, Bell, Colin** and **Thurcott, Anne.** Power, Persistence and Change. *A Second Study of Banbury. 196 pp.*

RURAL SOCIOLOGY

Mayer, Adrian C. Peasants in the Pacific. *A Study of Fiji Indian Rural Society. 248 pp. 20 plates.*

Williams, W. M. The Sociology of an English Village: *Gosforth. 272 pp. 12 figures. 13 tables.*

SOCIOLOGY OF INDUSTRY AND DISTRIBUTION

Dunkerley, David. The Foreman. *Aspects of Task and Structure. 192 pp.*

Eldridge, J. E. T. Industrial Disputes. *Essays in the Sociology of Industrial Relations. 288 pp.*

Hollowell, Peter G. The Lorry Driver. *272 pp.*

● **Oxaal, I., Barnett, T.** and **Booth, D.** (Eds) Beyond the Sociology of Development.

Economy and Society in Latin America and Africa. 295 pp.

Smelser, Neil J. Social Change in the Industrial Revolution: *An Application of Theory to the Lancashire Cotton Industry, 1770–1840. 468 pp. 12 figures. 14 tables.*

Watson, T. J. The Personnel Managers. *A Study in the Sociology of Work and Employment, 262 pp.*

ANTHROPOLOGY

Brandel-Syrier, Mia. Reeftown Elite. *A Study of Social Mobility in a Modern African Community on the Reef. 376 pp.*

Dickie-Clark, H. F. The Marginal Situation. *A Sociological Study of a Coloured Group. 236 pp.*

Dube, S. C. Indian Village. *Foreword by Morris Edward Opler. 276 pp. 4 plates.*
India's Changing Villages: *Human Factors in Community Development. 260 pp. 8 plates. 1 map.*

Fei, H.-T. Peasant Life in China. *A Field Study of Country Life in the Yangtze Valley. With a foreword by Bronislaw Malinowski. 328 pp. 16 pp. plates.*

Firth, Raymond. Malay Fishermen. *Their Peasant Economy. 420 pp. 17 pp. plates.*

Gulliver, P. H. Social Control in an African Society: a Study of the Arusha, Agricultural Masai of Northern Tanganyika. *320 pp. 8 plates. 10 figures.*
Family Herds. *288 pp.*

Jarvie, Ian C. The Revolution in Anthropology. *268 pp.*

Little, Kenneth L. Mende of Sierra Leone. *308 pp. and folder.*
Negroes in Britain. *With a New Introduction and Contemporary Study by Leonard Bloom. 320 pp.*

Tambs-Lyche, H. London Patidars. *About 180 pp.*

Madan, G. R. Western Sociologists on Indian Society. *Marx, Spencer, Weber, Durkheim, Pareto. 384 pp.*

Mayer, A. C. Peasants in the Pacific. *A Study of Fiji Indian Rural Society. 248 pp.*

Meer, Fatima. Race and Suicide in South Africa. *325 pp.*

Smith, Raymond T. The Negro Family in British Guiana: *Family Structure and Social Status in the Villages. With a Foreword by Meyer Fortes. 314 pp. 8 plates. 1 figure. 4 maps.*

SOCIOLOGY AND PHILOSOPHY

Adriaansens, H. Talcott Parsons and the Conceptual Dilemma. *About 224 pp.*

Barnsley, John H. The Social Reality of Ethics. *A Comparative Analysis of Moral Codes. 448 pp.*

Diesing, Paul. Patterns of Discovery in the Social Sciences. *362 pp.*

● **Douglas, Jack D.** (Ed.) Understanding Everyday Life. *Toward the Reconstruction of Sociological Knowledge. Contributions by Alan F. Blum, Aaron W. Cicourel, Norman K. Denzin, Jack D. Douglas, John Heeren, Peter McHugh, Peter K. Manning, Melvin Power, Matthew Speier, Roy Turner, D. Lawrence Wieder, Thomas P. Wilson and Don H. Zimmerman. 370 pp.*

Gorman, Robert A. The Dual Vision. *Alfred Schutz and the Myth of Phenomenological Social Science. 240 pp.*

Jarvie, Ian C. Concepts and Society. *216 pp.*

Kilminster, R. Praxis and Method. *A Sociological Dialogue with Lukács, Gramsci and the Early Frankfurt School. 334 pp.*

● **Pelz, Werner.** The Scope of Understanding in Sociology. *Towards a More Radical Reorientation in the Social Humanistic Sciences. 283 pp.*

Roche, Maurice. Phenomenology, Language and the Social Sciences. *371 pp.*

Sahay, Arun. Sociological Analysis. *212 pp.*

● **Slater, P.** Origin and Significance of the Frankfurt School. *A Marxist Perspective. 185 pp.*

Spurling, L. Phenomenology and the Social World. *The Philosophy of Merleau-Ponty and its Relation to the Social Sciences. 222 pp.*
Wilson, H. T. The American Ideology. *Science, Technology and Organization as Modes of Rationality. 368 pp.*

International Library of Anthropology
General Editor Adam Kuper

● **Ahmed, A. S.** Millennium and Charisma Among Pathans. *A Critical Essay in Social Anthropology. 192 pp.*
　Pukhtun Economy and Society. *Traditional Structure and Economic Development. About 360 pp.*
Barth, F. Selected Essays. *Volume I. About 250 pp.* Selected Essays. *Volume II. About 250 pp.*
Brown, Paula. The Chimbu. *A Study of Change in the New Guinea Highlands. 151 pp.*
Foner, N. Jamaica Farewell. *200 pp.*
Gudeman, Stephen. Relationships, Residence and the Individual. *A Rural Panamanian Community. 288 pp. 11 plates, 5 figures, 2 maps, 10 tables.*
　The Demise of a Rural Economy. *From Subsistence to Capitalism in a Latin American Village. 160 pp.*
Hamnett, Ian. Chieftainship and Legitimacy. *An Anthropological Study of Executive Law in Lesotho. 163 pp.*
Hanson, F. Allan. Meaning in Culture. *127 pp.*
Hazan, H. The Limbo People. *A Study of the Constitution of the Time Universe Among the Aged. About 192 pp.*
Humphreys, S. C. Anthropology and the Greeks. *288 pp.*
Karp, I. Fields of Change Among the Iteso of Kenya. *140 pp.*
Lloyd, P. C. Power and Independence. *Urban Africans' Perception of Social Inequality. 264 pp.*
Parry, J. P. Caste and Kinship in Kangra. *352 pp. Illustrated.*
Pettigrew, Joyce. Robber Noblemen. *A Study of the Political System of the Sikh Jats. 284 pp.*
Street, Brian V. The Savage in Literature. *Representations of 'Primitive' Society in English Fiction, 1858–1920. 207 pp.*
Van Den Berghe, Pierre L. Power and Privilege at an African University. *278 pp.*

International Library of Phenomenology and Moral Sciences
General Editor John O'Neill

Apel, K.-O. Towards a Transformation of Philosophy. *308 pp.*
Bologh, R. W. Dialectical Phenomenology. *Marx's Method. 287 pp.*
Fekete, J. The Critical Twilight. *Explorations in the Ideology of Anglo-American Literary Theory from Eliot to McLuhan. 300 pp.*
Medina, A. Reflection, Time and the Novel. *Towards a Communicative Theory of Literature. 143 pp.*

International Library of Social Policy
General Editor Kathleen Jones

Bayley, M. Mental Handicap and Community Care. *426 pp.*
Bottoms, A. E. and McClean, J. D. Defendants in the Criminal Process. *284 pp.*
Bradshaw, J. The Family Fund. *An Initiative in Social Policy. About 224 pp.*

Butler, J. R. Family Doctors and Public Policy. *208 pp.*

Davies, Martin. Prisoners of Society. *Attitudes and Aftercare. 204 pp.*

Gittus, Elizabeth. Flats, Families and the Under-Fives. *285 pp.*

Holman, Robert. Trading in Children. *A Study of Private Fostering. 355 pp.*

Jeffs, A. Young People and the Youth Service. *160 pp.*

Jones, Howard and Cornes, Paul. Open Prisons. *288 pp.*

Jones, Kathleen. History of the Mental Health Service. *428 pp.*

Jones, Kathleen with **Brown, John, Cunningham, W. J., Roberts, Julian** and **Williams, Peter.** Opening the Door. *A Study of New Policies for the Mentally Handicapped. 278 pp.*

Karn, Valerie. Retiring to the Seaside. *400 pp. 2 maps. Numerous tables.*

King, R. D. and **Elliot, K. W.** Albany: Birth of a Prison—End of an Era. *394 pp.*

Thomas, J. E. The English Prison Officer since 1850: *A Study in Conflict. 258 pp.*

Walton, R. G. Women in Social Work. *303 pp.*

● **Woodward, J.** To Do the Sick No Harm. *A Study of the British Voluntary Hospital System to 1875. 234 pp.*

International Library of Welfare and Philosophy
General Editors   Noel Timms and David Watson

● **McDermott, F. E.** (Ed.) Self-Determination in Social Work. *A Collection of Essays on Self-determination and Related Concepts by Philosophers and Social Work Theorists. Contributors: F. P. Biestek, S. Bernstein, A. Keith-Lucas, D. Sayer, H. H. Perelman, C. Whittington, R. F. Stalley, F. E. McDermott, I. Berlin, H. J. McCloskey, H. L. A. Hart, J. Wilson, A. I. Melden, S. I. Benn. 254 pp.*

● **Plant, Raymond.** Community and Ideology. *104 pp.*

Ragg, Nicholas M. People Not Cases. *A Philosophical Approach to Social Work. 168 pp.*

● **Timms, Noel** and **Watson, David.** (Eds) Talking About Welfare. *Readings in Philosophy and Social Policy. Contributors: T. H. Marshall, R. B. Brandt, G. H. von Wright, K. Nielsen, M. Cranston, R. M. Titmuss, R. S. Downie, E. Telfer, D. Donnison, J. Benson, P. Leonard, A. Keith-Lucas, D. Walsh, I. T. Ramsey. 320 pp.*

● Philosophy in Social Work. *250 pp.*

● **Weale, A.** Equality and Social Policy. *164 pp.*

Library of Social Work
General Editor   Noel Timms

● **Baldock, Peter.** Community Work and Social Work. *140 pp.*

○ **Beedell, Christopher.** Residential Life with Children. *210 pp. Crown 8vo.*

● **Berry, Juliet.** Daily Experience in Residential Life. *A Study of Children and their Care-givers. 202 pp.*

○ Social Work with Children. *190 pp. Crown 8vo.*

● **Brearley, C. Paul.** Residential Work with the Elderly. *116 pp.*

● Social Work, Ageing and Society. *126 pp.*

● **Cheetham, Juliet.** Social Work with Immigrants. *240 pp. Crown 8vo.*

● **Cross, Crispin P.** (Ed.) Interviewing and Communication in Social Work. *Contributions by C. P. Cross, D. Laurenson, B. Strutt, S. Raven. 192 pp. Crown 8vo.*

● **Curnock, Kathleen** and **Hardiker, Pauline**. Towards Practice Theory. *Skills and Methods in Social Assessments. 208 pp.*

● **Davies, Bernard.** The Use of Groups in Social Work Practice. *158 pp.*

● **Davies, Martin.** Support Systems in Social Work. *144 pp.*

Ellis, June. (Ed.) West African Families in Britain. *A Meeting of Two Cultures. Contributions by Pat Stapleton, Vivien Biggs. 150 pp. 1 Map.*

● **Hart, John.** Social Work and Sexual Conduct. *230 pp.*

● **Hutten, Joan M.** Short-Term Contracts in Social Work. *Contributions by Stella M. Hall, Elsie Osborne, Mannie Sher, Eva Sternberg, Elizabeth Tuters. 134 pp.*

Jackson, Michael P. and **Valencia, B. Michael.** Financial Aid Through Social Work. *140 pp.*

● **Jones, Howard.** The Residential Community. *A Setting for Social Work. 150 pp.*

● (Ed.) Towards a New Social Work. *Contributions by Howard Jones, D. A. Fowler, J. R. Cypher, R. G. Walton, Geoffrey Mungham, Philip Priestley, Ian Shaw, M. Bartley, R. Deacon, Irwin Epstein, Geoffrey Pearson. 184 pp.*

Jones, Ray and **Pritchard, Colin.** (Eds) Social Work With Adolescents. *Contributions by Ray Jones, Colin Pritchard, Jack Dunham, Florence Rossetti, Andrew Kerslake, John Burns, William Gregory, Graham Templeman, Kenneth E. Reid, Audrey Taylor. About 170 pp.*

○ **Jordon, William.** The Social Worker in Family Situations. *160 pp. Crown 8vo.*

● **Laycock, A. L.** Adolescents and Social Work. *128 pp. Crown 8vo.*

● **Lees, Ray.** Politics and Social Work. *128 pp. Crown 8vo.*

● Research Strategies for Social Welfare. *112 pp. Tables.*

○ **McCullough, M. K.** and **Ely, Peter J.** Social Work with Groups. *127 pp. Crown 8vo.*

● **Moffett, Jonathan.** Concepts in Casework Treatment. *128 pp. Crown 8vo.*

Parsloe, Phyllida. Juvenile Justice in Britain and the United States. *The Balance of Needs and Rights. 336 pp.*

● **Plant, Raymond.** Social and Moral Theory in Casework. *112 pp. Crown 8vo.*

Priestley, Philip, Fears, Denise and **Fuller, Roger.** Justice for Juveniles. *The 1969 Children and Young Persons Act: A Case for Reform? 128 pp.*

● **Pritchard, Colin** and **Taylor, Richard.** Social Work: Reform or Revolution? *170 pp.*

○ **Pugh, Elisabeth.** Social Work in Child Care. *128 pp. Crown 8vo.*

● **Robinson, Margaret.** Schools and Social Work. *282 pp.*

○ **Ruddock, Ralph.** Roles and Relationships. *128 pp. Crown 8vo.*

● **Sainsbury, Eric.** Social Diagnosis in Casework. *118 pp. Crown 8vo.*

● Social Work with Families. *Perceptions of Social Casework among Clients of a Family Service. 188 pp.*

Seed, Philip. The Expansion of Social Work in Britain. *128 pp. Crown 8vo.*

● **Shaw, John.** The Self in Social Work. *124 pp.*

Smale, Gerald G. Prophecy, Behaviour and Change. *An Examination of Self-fulfilling Prophecies in Helping Relationships. 116 pp. Crown 8vo.*

Smith, Gilbert. Social Need. *Policy, Practice and Research. 155 pp.*

● Social Work and the Sociology of Organisations. *124 pp. Revised edition.*

● **Sutton, Carole.** Psychology for Social Workers and Counsellors. *An Introduction. 248 pp.*

● **Timms, Noel.** Language of Social Casework. *122 pp. Crown 8vo.*

● Recording in Social Work. *124 pp. Crown 8vo.*

● **Todd, F. Joan.** Social Work with the Mentally Subnormal. *96 pp. Crown 8vo.*

● **Walrond-Skinner, Sue.** Family Therapy. *The Treatment of Natural Systems. 172 pp.*

● **Warham, Joyce.** An Introduction to Administration for Social Workers. *Revised edition. 112 pp.*

◑ An Open Case. *The Organisational Context of Social Work. 172 pp.*

○ **Wittenberg, Isca Salzberger.** Psycho-Analytic Insight and Relationships. *A Kleinian Approach. 196 pp. Crown 8vo.*

Primary Socialization, Language and Education

General Editor   Basil Bernstein

Adlam, Diana S., *with the assistance of Geoffrey Turner and Lesley Lineker.* Code in Context. *272 pp.*

Bernstein, Basil. Class, Codes and Control. *3 volumes.*
- 1. *Theoretical Studies Towards a Sociology of Language. 254 pp.*
    2. *Applied Studies Towards a Sociology of Language. 377 pp.*
- 3. *Towards a Theory of Educational Transmission. 167 pp.*

Brandis, W. and **Bernstein, B.** Selection and Control. *176 pp.*

Brandis, Walter and **Henderson, Dorothy.** Social Class, Language and Communication. *288 pp.*

Cook-Gumperz, Jenny. Social Control and Socialization. *A Study of Class Differences in the Language of Maternal Control. 290 pp.*

- **Gahagan, D. M.** and **G. A.** Talk Reform. *Exploration in Language for Infant School Children. 160 pp.*

Hawkins, P. R. Social Class, the Nominal Group and Verbal Strategies. *About 220 pp.*

Robinson, W. P. and **Rackstraw, Susan D. A.** A Question of Answers. *2 volumes. 192 pp. and 180 pp.*

Turner, Geoffrey J. and **Mohan, Bernard A.** A Linguistic Description and Computer Programme for Children's Speech. *208 pp.*

Reports of the Institute of Community Studies

Baker, J. The Neighbourhood Advice Centre. *A Community Project in Camden. 320 pp.*

- **Cartwright, Ann.** Patients and their Doctors. *A Study of General Practice. 304 pp.*

Dench, Geoff. Maltese in London. *A Case-study in the Erosion of Ethnic Consciousness. 302 pp.*

Jackson, Brian and **Marsden, Dennis.** Education and the Working Class: *Some General Themes Raised by a Study of 88 Working-class Children in a Northern Industrial City. 268 pp. 2 folders.*

Marris, Peter. The Experience of Higher Education. *232 pp. 27 tables.*
- Loss and Change. *192 pp.*

Marris, Peter and **Rein, Martin.** Dilemmas of Social Reform. *Poverty and Community Action in the United States. 256 pp.*

Marris, Peter and **Somerset, Anthony.** African Businessmen. *A Study of Entrepreneurship and Development in Kenya. 256 pp.*

Mills, Richard. Young Outsiders: *a Study in Alternative Communities. 216 pp.*

Runciman, W. G. Relative Deprivation and Social Justice. *A Study of Attitudes to Social Inequality in Twentieth-Century England. 352 pp.*

Willmott, Peter. Adolescent Boys in East London. *230 pp.*

Willmott, Peter and **Young, Michael.** Family and Class in a London Suburb. *202 pp. 47 tables.*

Young, Michael and **McGeeney, Patrick.** Learning Begins at Home. *A Study of a Junior School and its Parents. 128 pp.*

Young, Michael and **Willmott, Peter.** Family and Kinship in East London. *Foreword by Richard M. Titmuss. 252 pp. 39 tables.*
- The Symmetrical Family. *410 pp.*

Reports of the Institute for Social Studies in Medical Care

Cartwright, Ann, Hockey, Lisbeth and Anderson, John J. Life Before Death. *310 pp.*
Dunnell, Karen and Cartwright, Ann. Medicine Takers, Prescribers and Hoarders. *190 pp.*
Farrell, C. My Mother Said. . . *A Study of the Way Young People Learned About Sex and Birth Control. 288 pp.*

Medicine, Illness and Society
General Editor W. M. Williams

Hall, David J. Social Relations & Innovation. *Changing the State of Play in Hospitals. 232 pp.*
Hall, David J. and Stacey, M. (Eds) Beyond Separation. *234 pp.*
Robinson, David. The Process of Becoming Ill. *142 pp.*
Stacey, Margaret *et al.* Hospitals, Children and Their Families. *The Report of a Pilot Study. 202 pp.*
Stimson, G. V. and Webb, B. Going to See the Doctor. *The Consultation Process in General Practice. 155 pp.*

Monographs in Social Theory
General Editor Arthur Brittan

● Barnes, B. Scientific Knowledge and Sociological Theory. *192 pp.*
Bauman, Zygmunt. Culture as Praxis. *204 pp.*
● Dixon, Keith. Sociological Theory. *Pretence and Possibility. 142 pp.*
The Sociology of Belief. *Fallacy and Foundation. About 160 pp.*
Goff, T. W. Marx and Mead. *Contributions to a Sociology of Knowledge. 176 pp.*
Meltzer, B. N., Petras, J. W. and Reynolds, L. T. Symbolic Interactionism. *Genesis, Varieties and Criticisms. 144 pp.*
● Smith, Anthony D. The Concept of Social Change. *A Critique of the Functionalist Theory of Social Change. 208 pp.*

Routledge Social Science Journals

The British Journal of Sociology. *Editor – Angus Stewart; Associate Editor – Leslie Sklair. Vol. 1, No. 1 – March 1950 and Quarterly. Roy. 8vo. All back issues available. An international journal publishing original papers in the field of sociology and related areas.*
Community Work. *Edited by David Jones and Marjorie Mayo. 1973. Published annually.*
Economy and Society. *Vol. 1, No. 1. February 1972 and Quarterly. Metric Roy. 8vo. A journal for all social scientists covering sociology, philosophy, anthropology, economics and history. All back numbers available.*

Ethnic and Racial Studies. *Editor – John Stone. Vol. 1 – 1978. Published quarterly.*
Religion. Journal of Religion and Religions. *Chairman of Editorial Board, Ninian Smart. Vol. 1, No. 1, Spring 1971. A journal with an inter-disciplinary approach to the study of the phenomena of religion. All back numbers available.*
Sociology of Health and Illness. *A Journal of Medical Sociology. Editor – Alan Davies; Associate Editor – Ray Jobling. Vol. 1, Spring 1979. Published 3 times per annum.*
Year Book of Social Policy in Britain. *Edited by Kathleen Jones. 1971. Published annually.*

Social and Psychological Aspects of Medical Practice
Editor Trevor Silverstone

Lader, Malcolm. Psychophysiology of Mental Illness. *280 pp.*
● **Silverstone, Trevor** and **Turner, Paul.** Drug Treatment in Psychiatry. *Revised edition. 256 pp.*
Whiteley, J. S. and **Gordon, J.** Group Approaches in Psychiatry. *240 pp.*